# FOUR SEASONS COOKERY

## LESLEY WATERS

BBC BOOKS

Published by BBC Books,
a division of BBC Enterprises Limited,
Woodlands, 80 Wood Lane, London W12 OTT

First published 1992
© Lesley Waters 1992
The moral right of the author has been asserted

ISBN 0 563 36340 1

Designed by Sara Kidd
Illustrations © Vicky Emptage
Photographs © Matthew May
Home Economist Ricky Turner

Set in Bembo by Redwood Press Ltd, Melksham
Printed and bound in Great Britain by Clays Ltd, St Ives plc
Cover printed by Clays Ltd, St Ives plc

# CONTENTS

# ACKNOWLEDGEMENTS

Once again many thanks to Erica Griffiths and Susan Martineau for their continued support and input.

Very special thanks go to my sister Jacky Waters and to Declan Clark for all their hard work on the book and unfaltering encouragement throughout!

Last but never least, I'm grateful to Mum, Dad, Nan, Gaz and the Tims for being brave guinea pigs with good appetites.

# INTRODUCTION

Any good chef will tell you that to cook good food you need fine ingredients. But using the best fruit, vegetables and salads will not necessarily involve great expense – in fact it usually means the opposite. To buy the best all you need to do is to buy what is in season. Strawberry mousse made from tinned or frozen strawberries is never as good as that made from the fresh sun-ripened fruit which is abundant in the summer months. This book is about cooking cheaply and with the best available ingredients so *your* cooking can be economical but interesting.

Ever since I can remember, I've always loved home cooking – which means using fresh ingredients wherever possible and not tins and packets. Apart from the fact that it's healthier because you can cut down on additives, colourings and preservatives, it also means that what you cook tastes better and is more satisfying. The recipes that I've created for this book are very tasty – and they are also healthy and easy to make.

The book is divided into four main sections – one for each of the seasons of the year – and four extra parts which cover sauces, preserves, dressings and relishes. In each of the four main sections there are four sorts of recipes: lunches or light suppers; main meals; puddings; and 'specials'.

To create a meal for a family of four for under £5 all you have to do is choose a light or main meal, and add a pudding. Any combination of two dishes will only cost £5 for four people.

If you are a smaller family or if there are only two of you then halve the recipes to make a smaller amount. Alternatively, you can make more and follow the tips for using left-overs to create a new dish for the next day. Look out for the bowl and spoon symbol which indicates a recipe that uses left-overs to make a new meal.

The 'specials', as their name suggests, are recipes which can be used for special occasions and for entertaining your family and friends – from children's parties to a Christmas dinner. And of course, if you want to entertain a larger group than four all you have to do is to increase the amounts in the recipe to suit your needs.

The four final sections on sauces, preserves, dressings and relishes should help you make the most of gluts of fruit and vegetables so you have natural flavourings which you can store all year round in the freezer or just for a few days in the fridge. The sweet sauces have the added bonus of making excellent sorbets if they're frozen – especially refreshing for the summer months.

The recipes themselves have been inspired by national dishes from all around the world. They include Italian, Arabic and Greek dishes as well as barbecue and vegetarian food – so there's something for everyone. If you're conscious of trying to eat healthily I can guarantee that these recipes do not use pounds of sugar or pints of oil, but neither do they contain mountains of tofu and brown rice!

Today, it's all too easy to forget the seasonal pattern of fruit and vegetable harvests. Modern supermarkets with fresh produce imported from around the world can provide us with almost anything all year round – if we can afford it! But by following the guides at the beginning of each section about what is in season you can look out for the best buys. If you're unsure, visit your local greengrocer for the best value produce – at least you won't be paying for the packaging – which you can't eat! Also, it's worth keeping an eye open for fish in season. We often forget that certain seafood is more abundant at some times than others and it makes a wonderful, tasty change to meat. As I said at the beginning, I've always loved home cooking especially when it doesn't take all evening to prepare and all day to shop for! So the store-cupboard list on the next page will help you to keep basic foods at hand for cooking the recipes in this book so you only need to buy fruit, vegetables and meat or fish to make a meal. Enjoy your cooking!

# THE ALL-YEAR-ROUND STORE-CUPBOARD

A well-stocked store-cupboard is the key to easy cooking. Build up your stores gradually, adding a few things every week or month. In the end, your cupboard will save you time and money and will allow you to be more creative and spontaneous in the kitchen.

## GRAINS, PULSES AND BAKING PRODUCTS

Cracked wheat
Oatmeal
Porridge oats
Rice
Butter beans
Lentils
Pearl barley
Red kidney beans (tinned)
Dried pasta: Chinese egg noodles, pasta shapes, wholemeal spaghetti, macaroni, tagliatelli

Baking powder
Bicarbonate of soda
Cocoa powder
Cornflour
Flour: wholemeal, granary, plain, self-raising
Rice flour
Semolina

## FRUITS, NUTS AND SEEDS

Desiccated coconut
Dried fruits: apricots, prunes, dates, raisins, sultanas

Nuts: flaked almonds, ground almonds, walnuts, peanuts
Seeds: poppy, pumpkin, sesame, sunflower

## FLAVOURINGS AND SPICES

Chilli sauce
Garlic purée
Mint sauce
Mustard: English, French and
  wholegrain
Soy sauce
Tabasco sauce
Tikka or tandoori paste
Tomato purée
Vanilla essence
Vegetable stock cubes
Worcestershire sauce

Dried herbs: basil, bay leaves, dill
  weed and seed, marjoram,
  mixed herbs, oregano, sage,
  thyme
Dried spices: cayenne pepper,
  chilli powder, ground cinnamon,
  ground coriander, curry powder,
  garam masala, ground ginger,
  ground mixed spice, whole
  mustard seeds, whole nutmeg,
  paprika, turmeric

## SUGAR AND HONEY

Brown sugar
Caster sugar
Demerara sugar

Icing sugar
Honey

## CARTON AND TINNED GOODS

Fruit in natural juice (keep in a
  few of your favourites)
Sweetcorn
Whole and chopped tomatoes
Chopped tomatoes with herbs

Sieved tomatoes (in tins or
  cartons)
Creamed tomatoes
Tuna fish

## BOTTLED AND TINNED JUICES

Apple juice
Bottled lemon juice

Orange juice

## MISCELLANEOUS

Crunchy peanut butter
Dried wholemeal breadcrumbs
Eggs
Fromage frais
Muesli
Sunflower margarine or butter

Semi-skimmed milk (whole milk
  for children under 5)
Yoghurt
Sunflower oil
Wine vinegar

# SPRING

The arrival of spring brings a welcome change in the form of longer days and lighter nights. However, in early spring we still need to rely on winter vegetables and fruits although the first young carrots, broad beans, new potatoes, spinach, turnips, salad ingredients and fresh herbs are gradually creeping back into season. Turnips and beetroot are still cheap and plentiful but leave the beetroot off the salad plate and try it as a main ingredient in a tasty savoury gratin dish. Tender young spinach leaves and broad beans make an unusual crisp spring salad – try it with one of the simple dressings (pp. 121-123) which will add extra zing.

At this time of year fruit is still mainly imported and the cheapest fruits around will still be apples, pears and bananas. Fresh pineapple is widely available at this time of year and towards the end of May, gooseberries and apricots are just coming into season. As an alternative to fresh fruit salad try using a selection of dried fruits such as figs, apricots, prunes, peaches (see the recipe for Indian Tea Fruit Salad p. 26).

Keep a look out for mussels at this time of year as they are nearing the end of their season in early spring and are consequently very cheap. They are at their best steamed and combined with pasta dishes or in hot fish broths served with plenty of granary bread.

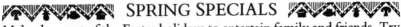 # SPRING SPECIALS

Make the most of the Easter holidays to entertain family and friends. Try the lamb and apricot pie for something a little special, or treat the children to the crocodile snap snack feast.

## EASTER SPECIAL
### SPRING LAMB PIE WITH SAVOURY FONDANT POTATOES AND STEAMED VEGETABLES (p. 29)

## CHILDREN'S TEATIME TREATS
### CROCODILE SNAP SNACK (p. 31)

### BEAR PAW BANANA, ICE-CREAM (p. 32)

## SEASONAL VEGETABLES

| | | |
|---|---|---|
| Avocado pears | Carrots | Salad ingredients |
| Beetroot | Cauliflower | Spinach |
| Broad beans | Courgettes | Spring greens |
| Broccoli | Leeks | Turnips |
| Butter beans | Mushrooms | |
| Cabbage | New potatoes | |

## SEASONAL FRUITS

| | | |
|---|---|---|
| Apples | Gooseberries | Pears |
| Apricots | Grapefruit | Pineapples |
| Bananas | Grapes | Rhubarb |

## SEASONAL FISH

| | |
|---|---|
| Mackerel | Mussels |

SPRING

# LIGHT SUPPERS AND LUNCHES

BROCCOLI BORSCH

LEEK AND BEETROOT GRATIN

SPRING MUSSEL BROTH

SMOKED MACKEREL KEDGEREE WITH HORSERADISH
AND ORANGE DRESSING

SPINACH AND BROAD BEAN SALAD WITH CARROT AND
PEANUT ROUND

MEXICAN HAM CORN CAKES WITH A TOMATO RELISH

## BROCCOLI BORSCH

'Borsch' normally refers to the beetroot and cabbage soup served in Russia. However, my version achieves a similar thick texture using broccoli and peas.

SERVES 4
*8 oz (225 g) broccoli*
*1 tablespoon sunflower oil*
*1 large onion, peeled and chopped*
*8 oz (225 g) frozen peas*
*1 teaspoon ground ginger*
*1 bay leaf*
*1½ pints (900 ml) vegetable or chicken stock*
*Freshly ground black pepper*
*½ Cos lettuce, washed and dried*
*2 teaspoons poppy seeds*
*1 tablespoon lemon juice*
*5 fl oz (150 ml) natural yoghurt*

Cut the broccoli into florets and slice the stalks thinly. In a saucepan, heat the oil and gently fry the onion until soft. Stir in the broccoli, peas, ginger and bay leaf and pour in the stock. Season well. Bring the contents of the saucepan to the boil, cover and simmer the soup for 20–25 minutes.

Meanwhile, shred the lettuce finely, toss it with the poppy seeds and lemon juice and set to one side.

Purée the cooked soup in a blender. Check the seasoning and adjust as necessary. Ladle the soup into large soup bowls. Add a pile of the salad to each bowl and drizzle over the yoghurt. Serve at once.

## *GREEN JACKETS*

Try these Russian-style potatoes with any left-over soup – you will find that left-over broccoli borsch thickens up.

Split some baked jacket potatoes and place on large plates ready to serve. Spoon over some of the hot, thick soup and top this with a spoonful of fromage frais and lots of freshly ground black pepper.

# LEEK AND BEETROOT GRATIN

A lively and tasty way to serve the much underrated beetroot.

### SERVES 4
*1 tablespoon sunflower oil*
*1 lb (450 g) leeks, washed and shredded*
*3 slices granary or wholemeal bread*
*1 lb (450 g) beetroot, cooked and sliced*
*Freshly ground black pepper*
*1 large egg*
*8 oz (225 g) fromage frais*
*2 tablespoons dried wholemeal breadcrumbs*
*2 oz (50 g) strong Cheddar cheese, grated*
*2 tablespoons chopped parsley*
*1 large clove garlic, peeled and halved*
*Knob of butter*

Pre-heat the grill.

In a frying-pan, heat the oil and gently cook the shredded leeks for 3–4 minutes or until softened. Toast the slices of bread under the grill.

Remove the leeks from the heat and toss in the sliced cooked beetroot. Season with plenty of black pepper and pile the mixture into a shallow ovenproof dish.

In a mixing bowl, beat together the egg and fromage frais. Season well.

Drizzle the egg mixture over the vegetables. Scatter with the breadcrumbs, cheese and parsley, place under the grill and cook for 6–8 minutes or until hot, crisp and golden-brown (reducing the heat if necessary).

Meanwhile, remove the crusts from the toasted bread, rub with the cut sides of the garlic clove and lightly butter. Cut each slice into 4 triangles.

Remove the gratin from the grill and surround with the toasted croûtons. Serve at once.

# SPRING MUSSEL BROTH

Serve crusty bread to mop up all the delicious juices of this simple fish stew.

### SERVES 4
*3 lb (1.5 kg) fresh mussels*
*1 tablespoon sunflower oil*
*1 large onion, peeled and chopped*
*2 tablespoons chopped parsley*
*1 clove garlic, peeled and crushed (optional)*
*1 bay leaf*
*10 fl oz (300 ml) apple juice*
*5 fl oz (150 ml) vegetable stock*
*Freshly ground black pepper*
*Knob of butter*

Clean the mussels by scrubbing and soaking well in cold water. Pull away all the seaweed threads. Discard any mussels which are cracked or which remain open when tapped.

In a large saucepan, heat the oil and gently fry the onion for 1 minute. Add the mussels and half the parsley together with the garlic (if using), bay leaf, apple juice and stock.

Season well. Cover the pan tightly with a lid and leave to steam over a medium heat for 5–7 minutes or until the mussel shells open.

Set a colander over a large pan and tip the mussels into the colander. Throw away any mussels which have not opened. Divide the mussels between 4 large soup bowls and cover with aluminium foil to keep warm.

Place the pan of mussel stock over a fierce heat and add the butter and remaining parsley. Bring to the boil and pour the stock over the mussels. Serve at once with lots of crusty bread.

# SMOKED MACKEREL KEDGEREE
## with horseradish and orange dressing

Kedgeree originates from an Indian dish which the Victorians brought back and adapted as a recipe eaten for breakfast. However, this version of kedgeree makes a super starter or a light lunch dish.

### SERVES 4
*2 tablespoons sunflower oil*
*1 large onion, peeled and chopped*
*3 teaspoons turmeric or curry powder*
*Juice of 1 lemon*
*8 oz (225 g) brown rice*
*8 oz (225 g) smoked mackerel fillet, skinned and flaked*
*2 tablespoons chopped parsley*
*FOR THE HORSERADISH AND ORANGE DRESSING*
*2 tablespoons horseradish cream*
*Juice and grated rind of 1 large orange*
*3 tablespoons fromage frais*
*Freshly ground black pepper*

In a frying-pan, heat the oil and gently fry the onion for 3–4 minutes. Reduce the heat, sprinkle in the turmeric or curry powder and cook for a further minute. Pour in the lemon juice and stir in the cooked rice. Fry very gently for a further 6–7 minutes, stirring occasionally.

In a mixing bowl, combine the horseradish, orange juice and rind and fromage frais. Season to taste and set to one side.

Finally, fold the flaked mackerel into the rice and heat through. Remove the kedgeree from the heat, pour over the dressing and serve from the pan, scattered with plenty of chopped parsley.

# SPINACH AND BROAD BEAN SALAD
## *with carrot and peanut round*

---

A most delicious way of serving broad beans, especially when accompanied by this nutty vegetable bread.

### SERVES 4–6
*8 oz (225 g) broad beans*
*12 oz (350 g) spinach, washed and torn into bite-size pieces*
*2 eggs, hard-boiled and chopped*
FOR THE DRESSING
*2 teaspoons French mustard*
*1 tablespoon white wine vinegar or lemon juice*
*1 clove garlic, crushed (optional)*
*2 tablespoons sunflower oil*
*4 tablespoons natural yoghurt*
*Freshly ground black pepper*
FOR THE CARROT AND PEANUT ROUND
*12 oz (350 g) wholemeal self-raising flour*
*4 oz (100 g) fine oatmeal*
*1 teaspoon bicarbonate of soda*
*1 oz (25 g) vegetable margarine*
*2 large carrots, peeled and grated*
*2 oz (50 g) peanuts, chopped*
*2 tablespoons chopped parsley*
*1 teaspoon dried thyme*
*1 small onion, peeled and finely chopped*
*5 fl oz (150 ml) skimmed milk*
*2 tablespoons natural yoghurt*
*1 tablespoon wholemeal flour*

Pre-heat the oven to gas mark 6, 400°F (200°C). Lightly grease a baking-tray.

First make the carrot and peanut round. In a large bowl, mix together the self-raising flour, oatmeal and soda. Using your fingertips, rub in the margarine. Mix in the carrots, peanuts, herbs and onion. Pour in the milk and yoghurt and quickly mix to a firm dough.

Dust a clean surface and your hands with flour, tip the dough on to the surface and knead for 30 seconds. Using your hands, shape the dough into an 8-inch (20-cm) round and place on the prepared baking-tray. Score the top with a knife into a lattice, sprinkle with the tablespoon of flour and bake in the oven for 30–35 minutes or until golden-brown (this bread will not rise as a normal loaf, but will have a scone-like appearance). Cool on a wire rack and serve warm.

To make the salad, plunge the broad beans into boiling water and cook for 4–5 minutes. Drain and refresh under cold water. Dry the washed spinach and toss with the broad beans and chopped hard-boiled eggs. Combine all the dressing ingredients together and season to taste. Pour the dressing over the salad and serve at once with the warm carrot and peanut round.

# MEXICAN HAM CORN CAKES
## with a tomato relish

Quick and easy, these can be whipped up in minutes. Especially good served with the relish. Left-over corn cakes make ideal fillers for packed lunches or are great toasted and served with baked beans.

### SERVES 4
*2 eggs*
*10 fl oz (300 ml) semi-skimmed milk*
*2 tablespoons sunflower oil*
*3 oz (75 g) plain flour*
*8 oz (225 g) cornmeal or semolina*
*1 teaspoon bicarbonate of soda*
*2 teaspoons salt*
*1 teaspoon chilli powder*
*1 × 8 oz (225 g) tin sweetcorn, drained*
*4 slices lean ham, chopped*

*FOR THE RELISH*
*2 large tomatoes, diced*
*1 teaspoon brown sugar*
*½ cucumber, grated*
*1 teaspoon white wine vinegar*
*7 oz (200 g) fromage frais*
*Freshly ground black pepper*
*1 punnet mustard and cress, washed and dried*

Pre-heat the oven to gas mark 6, 400°F (200°C). Lightly grease 12 wells of a patty tin.

In a bowl, beat the eggs, milk and oil together. Into a large mixing bowl, sift the flour, cornmeal or semolina, soda, salt and chilli powder. Gradually add the egg mixture and fold in the drained sweetcorn and chopped ham, taking care not to over-mix. Spoon the mixture into the greased patty tin – *do not smooth the tops*. Bake the cakes in the oven for 20–25 minutes or until puffed up and golden-brown.

Mix all the relish ingredients together and season to taste. Pour into a serving dish and scatter the mustard and cress over the top.

Tip the corn cakes out of the patty tin and serve in a bread basket with the relish. You could split the corn cakes for the relish to be spooned into the centre.

# Main Courses

### Pasta Paella

### Fish Cakes with Black-Eyed Beans served with Peasant Peas and New Potatoes Baked in their Skins

### Oaty Chicken with Lettuce and Watercress Dressing

### Oriental Vegetable Stew with Spiced Noodles and Orange and Onion Relish

### Celery Blue Cheese Bake with Savoury Fondant Potatoes and 'Simply Spinach'

## PASTA PAELLA

When we think of paella, rice immediately springs to mind. Here's a Spanish variation using macaroni which gives a lighter result.

SERVES 4

*1 large onion, chopped*
*2 tablespoons sunflower oil*
*1 clove garlic, peeled and crushed*
*1 teaspoon turmeric*
*2 teaspoons mild curry powder*
*3 large carrots, scrubbed and grated*
*12 oz (350 g) macaroni*
*1 pint (600 ml) chicken stock*
*1 bay leaf*
*1 piece orange rind*
*Freshly ground black pepper*
*1 large whiting, filleted and skinned*
*1 lb (450 g) fresh mussels, scrubbed and picked over*
*2 tablespoons chopped parsley*
*Warm crusty granary bread to serve*

In a large frying-pan or wok, fry the onion in the oil for 3 minutes until softened and golden. Stir in the garlic, turmeric and curry powder and cook for a further minute. Scatter over the grated carrots and macaroni and add the chicken stock, bay leaf and orange rind. Season with black pepper and bring to the boil. Cover, lower the heat and simmer for 20 minutes, adding extra stock if necessary.

Cut the whiting fillets into bite-size pieces. Prepare the mussels (see p. 13) – if you are using them – throwing away any which are cracked or which remain open when tapped. Add all the fish and shellfish to the paella, cover and cook for a further 6–7 minutes. Discard any mussels which have not opened after this time.

Scatter the paella with chopped parsley and serve at once with plenty of warm crusty bread. Usually this dish is served in its cooking pan, but you may choose to transfer it to a heated serving dish.

# FISH CAKES WITH BLACK-EYED BEANS
*served with peasant peas and new potatoes baked in their skins*

Mackerel has a good, strong flavour which works well for these fish cakes.

SERVES 4
*FOR THE FISH CAKES*
*1 lb (450 g) mackerel, filleted*
*2 eggs*
*1 × 14 oz (400 g) tin black-eyed beans, drained*
*Freshly grated nutmeg to taste*
*1 tablespoon soy sauce*
*1 teaspoon dried sage*
*¼ teaspoon chilli powder*
*Dried wholemeal breadcrumbs*
*1 tablespoon sunflower oil*
*FOR THE POTATOES*
*1 lb (450 g) unpeeled new potatoes, washed*
*2 tablespoons sunflower oil*
*1 teaspoon dried or 2 teaspoons chopped fresh thyme*
*Freshly ground black pepper*

## FOR THE PEASANT PEAS
*1 lb (450 g) frozen peas*
*Vegetable stock*
*1 medium onion, peeled and sliced*
*1 bay leaf*
*1 clove of garlic, peeled and crushed*
*1 teaspoon plain flour*

Pre-heat the oven to gas mark 5, 375°F (190°C).

Lightly grease an ovenproof dish or baking-tray. Place the mackerel fillet, skin side up, in the dish and barely cover it with boiling water. Bake in the oven for 8–10 minutes or until the fish is cooked and the skin comes away easily.

Parboil the potatoes in their skins for 6 minutes. Drain them well and place them on a large sheet of aluminium foil. Drizzle over the oil, scatter with the herbs and season well. Enclose the potatoes in the foil and seal the edges firmly. Place the parcel on a baking-sheet (you could use the dish in which the fish was cooked) and bake in the oven for 50 minutes to 1 hour or until the potatoes are tender.

Meanwhile, beat the eggs in a small bowl and set aside. In a large mixing bowl, use a fork to mash the black-eyed beans thoroughly. Add the nutmeg, soy sauce, sage, chilli, 1 tablespoon of the breadcrumbs and half the beaten eggs. Remove the skin from the cooked fish and flake the flesh into pieces. Combine with the bean mixture and allow to chill for 30 minutes.

On a lightly floured surface, divide the fish mixture into 8 roughly equal portions. Form each portion into a neat round. Brush the cakes with the remaining beaten egg and dip them into the remaining breadcrumbs to coat them on all sides. Place them on a lightly greased baking-tray, sprinkle any left-over breadcrumbs on top and drizzle over the sunflower oil. Bake in the oven for 30–40 minutes or until crisp and cooked through.

Fifteen minutes before serving, cover the peas with vegetable stock and add the onion, bay leaf and garlic. Simmer until the peas are tender. Mix the flour with 2 tablespoons of water. Add the flour paste to the peas and continue to simmer for 2–3 minutes or until the liquid thickens slightly. Season well and pile into a serving dish. Serve piping hot with the fish cakes and potatoes.

# OATY CHICKEN
## with lettuce, and watercress dressing

An attractive stir-fry of oaty chicken and mushrooms served on a bed of salad.

### SERVES 4
### FOR THE CHICKEN
*4 chicken thighs or drumsticks, boned*
*4 oz (100 g) mushrooms, wiped and thickly sliced*
*1 egg, beaten*
*4 oz (100 g) porridge oats*
*1 teaspoon ground coriander*
*1 teaspoon dried oregano*
*Freshly ground black pepper*
*1 tablespoon sunflower oil*
*1 large Cos lettuce, washed, dried and shredded*
### FOR THE WATERCRESS DRESSING
*1 bunch watercress, washed*
*1 tablespoon lemon juice*
*5 fl oz (150 ml) natural yoghurt*
*1 teaspoon mint sauce*
*Juice and grated rind of 1 orange*
*2 teaspoons French mustard*
*Freshly ground black pepper*

Cut the chicken into thin, finger-like strips and toss with the mushrooms in the beaten egg. In a roasting-tin, mix together the oats, coriander, oregano and black pepper. Add the chicken and mushrooms and coat with the herby oats.

Heat the oil in a frying-pan or wok and cook half the chicken and mushrooms for 10–12 minutes, tossing gently. Remove and keep warm while you cook the remainder.

Divide the shredded lettuce between 4 large plates. Liquidise the dressing ingredients together and season to taste.

Spoon the chicken over the lettuce and drizzle over a little of the dressing. Hand the remaining dressing separately. Serve hot.

# ORIENTAL VEGETABLE STEW
*with spiced noodles and orange and onion relish*

---

An oriental-style feast for you to try. Spaghetti or any pasta may be used in place of noodles.

### SERVES 4
### FOR THE VEGETABLE STEW
*1 tablespoon sunflower oil*
*1 large onion, peeled and chopped*
*1 small cauliflower, divided into florets*
*2 large carrots, scrubbed and thinly sliced*
*1 level teaspoon chilli powder or cayenne pepper*
*1 teaspoon ground ginger*
*Freshly ground black pepper*
*1 tablespoon desiccated coconut*
*1¼ pints (750 ml) vegetable stock*
*1 medium unpeeled potato, washed and grated*
*2 tablespoons fromage frais*
*Orange and onion relish (see p. 118) to serve*
### FOR THE SPICED NOODLES
*8 oz (225 g) dried pasta or Chinese egg noodles*
*1 tablespoon sunflower oil*
*1 clove garlic, peeled and crushed*
*2 teaspoons curry powder*
*1 tablespoon peanut butter*
*2 tablespoons soy sauce*
*10 fl oz (300 ml) water*
*8 oz (225 g) spring greens or spinach, washed and finely shredded*
*Freshly ground black pepper*

For the stew, heat the oil in a large saucepan, add the onion, cauliflower and carrots and sweat gently for 6 minutes. Sprinkle in the spices and cook for a further minute. Stir well and season with black pepper. Add the coconut, stock and grated potato. Cover and bring to the boil. Reduce the heat and simmer for 20–25 minutes.

Prepare the relish 30 minutes before serving (see p. 118).

Ten minutes before serving, plunge the noodles into boiling water and cook for about 5–6 minutes or until just tender. Drain thoroughly. Heat the oil in a large frying-pan or wok, toss in the cooked noodles and gently heat them through. In a bowl, mix together the garlic, curry powder, peanut butter, soy sauce and water and add these to the noodles, tossing well.

Just before serving, add the spring greens and seasoning to the noodles and stir the fromage frais into the vegetable stew. Serve very hot with the chilled relish.

# CELERY BLUE CHEESE BAKE
## with savoury fondant potatoes and 'simply spinach'

---

A delicious combination of celery and blue cheese: a nourishing filling meal.

### SERVES 4
### FOR THE CELERY BLUE CHEESE BAKE
*1 large head celery, washed, roughly chopped and leaves reserved*
*10 fl oz (300 ml) vegetable stock*
*15 fl oz (450 ml) semi-skimmed milk*
*4 oz (100 g) low-fat cream cheese*
*4 oz (100 g) blue cheese, grated*
*2 oz (50 g) flaked almonds*
*2 teaspoons French mustard*
*Freshly ground black pepper*
*2 tablespoons dried wholemeal breadcrumbs*
*Paprika*
### FOR THE SAVOURY FONDANT POTATOES (see p. 30)
### FOR THE 'SIMPLY SPINACH'
*8 oz (225 g) fresh spinach, washed and roughly chopped*
*1 tablespoon lemon juice*
*2 tablespoons sunflower oil*
*Freshly ground black pepper*

Pre-heat the oven to gas mark 4, 350°F (180°C).

Place the celery in a pan and cover with the stock. Bring to the boil and simmer for 12–15 minutes or until tender. Drain and reserve the stock.

In a bowl, beat together the milk, cream cheese, blue cheese, almonds, mustard and the reserved stock. Season with pepper. Fold in the celery and pile into an ovenproof dish. Scatter over the breadcrumbs and sprinkle with paprika. Place in the oven and bake for 1¼ hours until golden and bubbling.

Prepare the savoury fondant potatoes (see p. 30).

Wash and prepare the spinach. Just before serving, toss the spinach in the lemon juice and sunflower oil and season well. Pile into a salad bowl.

Remove the celery bake from the oven. Scatter with the chopped celery leaves and hand the salad and potatoes separately.

## CELERY, CHEESE AND HAM QUICHE

Left-over celery blue cheese bake can be transformed into a tasty filling for a savoury quiche. Simply add a couple of beaten eggs, 5 fl oz (150 ml) milk and 4 oz (100 g) chopped lean ham and combine thoroughly. Pile the mixture into a cooked pastry case and bake in the oven for about 20–25 minutes, or until firm.

# PUDDINGS

APPLE AMBER PUDDING

INDIAN TEA FRUIT SALAD

BANANA BRÛLÉE

GRILLED GRAPEFRUIT WITH PANCAKES

PINEAPPLE PASKHA FLAN

## APPLE AMBER PUDDING

A light bread and butter pudding with an unusual topping of apples and spices.

SERVES 4
*6–8 slices brown bread, buttered*
*3 eating apples, cored and thinly sliced*
*2 eggs*
*1 pint (600 ml) milk*
*2 tablespoons honey*
*2 teaspoons ground cinnamon*
*1 teaspoon freshly grated nutmeg*
*1 tablespoon brown sugar*

Pre-heat the oven to gas mark 4, 350°F (180°C). Lightly grease an oven-proof dish.

Cut the bread into fingers – do not remove the crust. Arrange the fingers in the baking dish – *buttered side up*. Scatter half the apple slices over the bread. In a bowl, beat together the eggs, milk and honey and pour this over the bread and apples. Set to one side and allow to stand for 30 minutes. After this time, scatter the remaining apples on the top. Mix the spices and brown sugar together and sprinkle over the pudding. Bake in the oven for 50 minutes or until the custard has set and the top is crisp and golden-brown. Serve warm.

# INDIAN TEA FRUIT SALAD

This salad makes a delicious pudding, especially when served with warm oatcakes or muesli-style biscuits and yoghurt. It's also great on top of cereal or porridge for breakfast or a brunch snack.

### SERVES 4
*8 oz (225 g) mixed dried fruit*
*4 oz (100 g) sultanas*
*10 coriander seeds, crushed (optional)*
*1 pint (600 ml) freshly made Indian tea*
*2 ripe bananas*
*Juice and grated rind of 1 large orange*

Place the dried fruit in a heatproof mixing bowl with the coriander seeds. Pour the hot tea over the mixture and allow to infuse overnight.

Peel and slice the bananas and add them to the salad along with the orange juice and rind. Leave to stand for at least an hour before serving.

# BANANA BRÛLÉE

Bananas and apricots with a caramelised topping. Best served chilled.

### SERVES 4
*3 ripe bananas, peeled and thickly sliced*
*1 × 7 oz (200 g) tin apricots, drained and sliced*
*1 lb (450 g) fromage frais*
*3 oz (75 g) demerara sugar*

Place the bananas and apricots in a shallow ovenproof dish. Spoon over and completely cover the fruit with the fromage frais. Place the dish in the freezer for 35–40 minutes.

Pre-heat the grill.

Remove the dish from the freezer and scatter evenly with demerara sugar. Place under the grill until the sugar has caramelised. Cool and chill until very cold – approximately 2 hours. Serve chilled.

# GRILLED GRAPEFRUIT WITH PANCAKES

Orange can be used in place of the grapefruit in this recipe; however, grapefruit makes a pleasant, refreshing change and goes particularly well with the pancakes.

SERVES 4
*2 grapefruit*
*2 tablespoons demerara sugar*
*9 oz (250 g) fromage frais*
*FOR THE PANCAKES*
*4 oz (100 g) wholemeal flour*
*1 tablespoon cocoa powder*
*1 large egg*
*2 teaspoons brown sugar*
*5 fl oz (150 ml) milk*
*A little sunflower oil for frying*

Lightly grease a baking-tray.

Using a sharp knife, remove the peel and pith from the grapefruit. Cut across the fruit to form thin slices and arrange these, overlapping, on the baking-tray. Place in the freezer for 15 minutes.

Meanwhile, make the pancakes. Sift the flour and cocoa powder into a large mixing bowl and make a well in the centre. Add the egg and sugar and half the milk. Beat the mixture until smooth, adding the remaining milk gradually. Set the batter to one side.

Pre-heat the grill.

To cook the pancakes, brush a little oil in a frying-pan and place over the heat. Drop spoonfuls of the batter on to the pan to form small pancakes and cook these on both sides. Continue in this way until you have used all the batter, keeping the pancakes warm on a foil-covered dinner plate.

Remove the grapefruit slices from the freezer. Sprinkle over the demerara sugar and place under the hot grill for 4–5 minutes or until the sugar has completely caramelised. Divide the pancakes between 4 warm plates and top each one with a spoonful of fromage frais and hot, sliced grapefruit and serve at once.

# PINEAPPLE PASKHA FLAN

Here we have a crisp pastry case filled with a cream cheese filling and topped with fresh pineapple.

SERVES 4
*8 oz (225 g) ready-made shortcrust pastry*
*½ fresh pineapple*
*1 × 8 oz (225 g) carton low-fat cream cheese or curd cheese*
*4 oz (100 g) sultanas*
*2 teaspoons vanilla essence*
*FOR THE GLAZE*
*2 tablespoons good-quality apricot jam*
*1 tablespoon water*

Pre-heat the oven to gas mark 6, 400°F (200°C). Lightly grease an 8-inch (20-cm) flan tin.

On a floured surface, roll out the pastry and line the flan tin with it. Allow the pastry to chill in the refrigerator for 15 minutes – this will allow it to 'relax' and so will help prevent shrinkage during cooking.

Prick the base of the flan case with a fork and cover with a sheet of greaseproof paper. Half-fill this with raw rice, dried pasta or dried beans. Bake the flan case 'blind' in the oven for 15–20 minutes or until almost cooked. Remove the paper and rice and return the pastry to the oven for a further 3 minutes or until completely cooked.

Prepare the pineapple by removing the hard skin and slicing the flesh thinly. Prepare the glaze by heating the jam and water together in a small saucepan, then set to one side.

Mix together the cream or curd cheese, sultanas and vanilla essence and spoon this mixture into the cooled flan base. Arrange the pineapple slices around the flan and lightly brush with the warm apricot glaze.

## PINEAPPLE PARCELS

This is a great way of using up pineapple left over from the previous recipe. Serve with almond biscuits (see p. 109).

SERVES 4
½ fresh pineapple
10 fl oz (300 ml) orange juice
1 teaspoon freshly grated nutmeg
4 oz (100 g) raisins or sultanas

Peel and chop the pineapple and marinate in the orange juice with the nutmeg and the raisins or sultanas for 30 minutes at room temperature.

Pre-heat the oven to gas mark 6, 400°F (200°C).

Divide the fruit and juice between 4 squares of aluminium foil and draw up the edges to seal carefully. Place the parcels on a baking-tray and bake for 10–12 minutes. Serve the parcels on individual dishes and allow each guest to open his or her own.

# EASTER SPECIAL

## SPRING LAMB PIE
### with savoury fondant potatoes and steamed vegetables

---

SERVES 4
FOR THE LAMB PIE
1 lb (450 g) ready-made shortcrust pastry
Milk to glaze
1 tablespoon sunflower oil
8 oz (225 g) lamb fillet, cut into thin slices
1½ oz (40 g) plain flour
8 oz (225 g) no-soak, dried apricots, cut in half
1 lb (450 g) parsnips, peeled and cut into thin sticks
1 teaspoon dried mixed herbs
1½ pints (900 ml) vegetable stock
1 bay leaf
Freshly ground black pepper
2 tablespoons fromage frais or natural yoghurt
FOR THE SAVOURY FONDANT POTATOES
1½ lb (750 g) medium potatoes
1 oz (25 g) butter
Chicken stock
Chopped parsley to garnish

## *FOR THE STEAMED VEGETABLES*
*1 lb (450 g) spring greens, shredded; or broccoli, divided into florets*

Pre-heat the oven to gas mark 6, 400°F (200°C).

Cut the potatoes in half and parboil for 6 minutes. Drain well. Put the potatoes into an ovenproof dish and add the butter and enough boiling chicken stock to half-cover them. Place the dish in the oven for 45 minutes – 1 hour to allow the potatoes to absorb the stock.

Meanwhile, lightly grease an 8-inch (20-cm) spring-sided flan tin or flan ring. On a floured surface, roll out about two-thirds of the pastry and use it to line the tin. Bake blind (see p. 28). Remove from the oven and keep warm.

Roll out the remaining pastry into a 9-inch (23-cm) round and tidy the edges to form a lid for the pie. Place this on a greased baking-tray and decorate by cutting a lattice pattern into the pastry. Brush the lid with milk and bake in the oven for 10–15 minutes or until golden and crisp. Remove from the oven and keep warm.

In a frying-pan or wok, heat the oil and fry the lamb over a fierce heat for 2–3 minutes. Sprinkle over the flour and cook for a further 30 seconds. Add the apricots, parsnips, herbs, vegetable stock and bay leaf. Stir these well together and bring to the boil. Reduce the heat and simmer gently for 40 minutes, adding extra liquid if required.

Fifteen minutes before serving, steam the spring greens or broccoli until just tender.

When you are ready to serve, remove the potatoes from the oven, turn them out into a heated serving dish and sprinkle with chopped parsley. Keep warm.

Season the lamb to taste and stir in the fromage frais or yoghurt at the last moment. Spoon the lamb filling into the warm pastry case (you can, if you wish, transfer the case to a large serving dish for the table) and arrange the cooked lid on top.

Serve the pie at once with the fondant potatoes and steamed spring greens or broccoli.

# CHILDREN'S TEATIME TREATS

## CROCODILE SNAP SNACK

SERVES 6–8 CHILDREN
1 wholemeal or granary French stick
1 lb (450 g) low-fat cream cheese
1 egg, hard-boiled and chopped
½ cucumber, grated
1 teaspoon yeast extract
Freshly ground black pepper
1 carrot, scrubbed and grated
1 punnet mustard and cress, washed and dried
1 × 7 oz (200 g) tin tuna fish, drained
2 tomatoes, chopped
1 tablespoon peanut butter
1 teaspoon water
1 slice ham
Peanuts
2 Olives or radishes
Lettuce leaves

Slit open one end of the French stick to resemble a mouth, as shown in the illustration. Cut down the length of the stick and open it out, lifting off the 'lid' as illustrated.

Divide the cream cheese equally between 3 bowls. To the first bowl add the chopped egg, cucumber and yeast extract and season to taste. In the second bowl, combine the grated carrot, cress and tuna fish and again

season to taste. In the third bowl, mix together the tomatoes, peanut butter and water and, once again, season.

Place the French stick on a large board or serving dish and spoon the 3 fillings into the 'back' or 'body' in separate sections. Replace the 'lid'. Roll the slice of ham and place it in the 'mouth' with peanuts each side to resemble a tongue and teeth. Add radishes or olives to resemble the eyes. Surround the 'crocodile' with lettuce leaves and serve by simply cutting into chunks.

# BEAR PAW BANANA ICE-CREAM

### SERVES 6–8 CHILDREN
*2 large ripe bananas, peeled and sliced*
*1 tablespoon runny honey*
*8 oz (225 g) fromage frais or 2 × 4 oz (100 g) cartons apricot yoghurt*
*2 teaspoons drinking chocolate powder to decorate*

In a blender, liquidise 1 banana with the honey and fromage frais or yoghurt. Turn this into an ice tray or shallow dish and place in the freezer until half-frozen through. Using a fork, mash the half-frozen mixture to a smooth paste and fold in the remaining banana slices. Return to the freezer until almost frozen through (though still a little slushy). This should take about 2 hours in all.

To serve the ice-cream, spoon it into bowls, dust with a little drinking chocolate powder and serve it with muesli-style biscuits.

# SUMMER

Summertime – and the shopping is easy!

Without a doubt summer gives the most abundant choice of fruit and vegetables. Hot, sunny weather (we hope) calls for a lighter approach to meal times, so heavy main courses tend to give way to more simply prepared dishes to tantalise and refresh your tastebuds.

Just for starters, tuck into warm chilli corn bread with Mexican dip or try a grilled kebab of new potatoes and baby beetroots, or Italian toasties with mushroom butter.

Marrows make an appearance at this time of year. They are notable for being a very adaptable vegetable as they can also be turned into chutney or jam, stuffed and baked, barbecued or quite simply steamed and served with one of the many dressings in the book (see pp. 121–123). Remember, when choosing a marrow go for the smaller ones which will have a better flavour and texture. As well as the 'Special' recipe, try fresh sardines, pilchards and trout on the barbecue using the chicken marinade recipe (p. 57) to baste them.

For the finishing touch, choose one of the simple puddings. Remember, do not be afraid to ring the changes with your own choice of soft summer fruit. This is the time to eat as much luscious fruit as you can and it's an ideal opportunity to make quick ice-creams, sorbets and instant jams or, alternatively, freeze your summer fruits and get the benefit from them when they are not in season.

# SUMMER SPECIALS

Warm summer nights give us the chance to eat alfresco – out of doors. Invite your family or friends for a special Midsummer Night's supper and make use of the barbecue if you have one. Serve the tangy chicken recipe, and use the barbecue right to the end with a pudding of bananas flamed in their skins.

## *BARBECUE SPECIALS*
### TANGY BARBECUED CHICKEN WITH GARLIC POTATOES IN FOIL, TOMATO AND APPLE RELISH AND 'SIMPLY SPINACH' (p. 57)

### BANANAS FLAMED IN THEIR SKINS (p. 58)

## *SEASONAL VEGETABLES*

| | | |
|---|---|---|
| Cauliflower | Green peas | Runner beans |
| Corn-on-the-cob | Marrow | Salad ingredients |
| Fennel | New potatoes | Spinach |
| Green beans | Peppers | Watercress |

## *SEASONAL FRUITS*

| | | |
|---|---|---|
| Apricots | Nectarines | Red water melon |
| Blackcurrants | Peaches | Rhubarb |
| Cherries | Plums | Strawberries |
| Gooseberries | Raspberries | |
| Loganberries | Redcurrants | |

## *SEASONAL FISH*

| | | |
|---|---|---|
| Haddock | Sardines | Trout |
| Pilchards | | |

# LIGHT SUPPERS AND LUNCHES

SUMMER VEGETABLES WITH CURRIED DRESSING

KING COS SALAD

SUMMER SOUP WITH SEEDY RELISH AND TOASTED CRACKERS

CHILLI CORN BREAD WITH MEXICAN DIP

NEW POTATO AND BEETROOT SKEWERS WITH GRAINY MUSTARD SAUCE

SUMMER SATAY

OMELETTE FLORENTINE

## SUMMER VEGETABLES
### *with curried dressing*

Attractive, summer-style vegetables with a spicy dressing – delicious accompanied by warm pitta bread or crusty rolls.

### SERVES 4
*1 lb (450 g) small unpeeled new potatoes, washed and scrubbed*
*1 lb (450 g) runner beans, prepared and sliced*
*1 tablespoon sunflower oil*
*1 bunch radishes, trimmed (halved if large)*
*½ cucumber, cut into sticks*
*1 teaspoon honey*
*1 tablespoon sesame seeds*
*Crisp lettuce leaves, washed and dried*

*FOR THE CURRIED DRESSING*
*4 tablespoons fromage frais*
*2 heaped teaspoons curry paste*
*Juice of 1 orange*
*1 teaspoon mint sauce*
*Freshly ground black pepper*

Plunge the potatoes into boiling water and cook for 15 minutes or until tender. Four minutes before the end of the cooking time add the runner beans to the pan.

Mix together the dressing ingredients, seasoning well.

Heat the oil in a large frying-pan or wok. Stir-fry the radishes and cucumber for 1 minute. Spoon on the honey and toss well together. Drain the potatoes and beans thoroughly and add them to the stir-fry pan. Lower the heat and sprinkle over the sesame seeds.

Divide the lettuce leaves between 4 plates and spoon the hot glazed vegetables on top. Drizzle over a little of the curried dressing and hand the rest separately. Serve at once.

# KING COS SALAD

This is a light, refreshing salad which is lovely accompanied by warm granary bread.

SERVES 4
*1 large Cos lettuce, washed and dried*
*2 large oranges*
*1 ripe avocado pear*
*4 rashers lean bacon, rinded and diced*
*2 slices wholemeal bread, diced*
*1 teaspoon dried mixed herbs*
*FOR THE CHEESY DRESSING*
*4 oz (100 g) low-fat cream cheese*
*3 tablespoons cold vegetable stock*
*2 tablespoons lemon juice*
*2 teaspoons wholegrain French mustard*
*Freshly ground black pepper*

Tear the lettuce into bite-size pieces and place it in a large salad bowl.

Using the fine part of a grater, remove the rind from the oranges and set to one side. With a sharp knife, cut the pith from the oranges and then cut the flesh horizontally into slices.

Cut the avocado in half, remove the stone, peel and cut the flesh into slices. Gently combine the orange and avocado with the lettuce and set to one side.

For the dressing, mix the dressing ingredients with the orange rind and season to taste.

In a large frying-pan, dry-fry the diced bacon until crisp. Add the diced bread and cook until well toasted. Sprinkle over the herbs. Remove the pan from the heat and spoon the hot bacon and croûtons over the salad. Spoon on the dressing, toss well and take the salad to the table at once.

# SUMMER SOUP
## with seedy relish and toasted crackers

Don't keep soup just for those cold winter days – it's just as tasty served chilled and is very refreshing.

### SERVES 4
1 clove garlic, peeled and crushed (optional)
1 cucumber, grated
2 teaspoons mint sauce
5 fl oz (150 ml) fromage frais
5 fl oz (150 ml) orange juice
10 fl oz (300 ml) vegetable stock
4 crisp salad leaves, washed, dried and shredded
Freshly ground black pepper
Cream crackers
Ice cubes to serve
### FOR THE SEEDY RELISH
2 large tomatoes, chopped
1 tablespoon sunflower seeds
2 teaspoons poppy seeds
Juice of 1 lemon

In a large bowl, mix together the first seven of the soup ingredients, including the garlic (if using), and season well. Cover and place in the refrigerator to chill for 2–3 hours. Meanwhile, combine the relish ingredients and pile into a glass serving dish.

Just before serving the soup, toast the crackers under the grill and keep warm in a basket. Ladle the soup into bowls with a few ice cubes and serve at once with the relish and warm crackers.

Left-over soup can be liquidised and kept in the refrigerator for use as a delicious dressing for salads and vegetables.

# CHILLI CORN BREAD
## *with Mexican dip*

This spicy bread is quick to make. Serve it straight from the oven with the Mexican dip or with salad, soups or casseroles. Freeze left-overs to use another time or try the corn bread pizzas on p. 39.

### SERVES 4–6
*10 oz (275 g) cornmeal or fine semolina*
*3 oz (75 g) plain flour*
*2 teaspoons bicarbonate of soda*
*1 teaspoon chilli powder*
*Freshly ground black pepper*
*1 egg*
*15 fl oz (450 ml) natural yoghurt*
*4 oz (100 g) fresh chilli peppers, washed, chopped and de-seeded, or*
*tinned chilli peppers, drained and chopped*
*1 × 14 oz (400 g) tin sweetcorn, drained*
*5 fl oz (150 ml) milk*
*4 tablespoons chopped parsley*
*FOR THE MEXICAN DIP*
*2 × 14 oz (400 g) tins tomatoes*
*1 large carrot, scrubbed and grated*
*2 teaspoons chilli powder*
*1 tablespoon tomato purée*
*1 clove garlic, peeled and crushed*
*Freshly ground black pepper*

Pre-heat the oven to gas mark 6, 400°F (200°C). Grease a 10-inch (25-cm) square loaf-tin or small roasting-tin.

In a large bowl, mix together the cornmeal or semolina, flour, soda, and black pepper. Either add the chilli powder to these dry ingredients or add the chopped chillis to the wet mixture. In a jug, beat together the egg, yoghurt, sweetcorn, milk and parsley. Pour this mixture over the flour and combine thoroughly. Transfer the dough to the loaf-tin and bake in the oven for 25–30 minutes or until firm and golden on top.

In a saucepan, mix together the dip ingredients and heat through. Cover and simmer for 20–25 minutes or until thickened, seasoning to taste. Pour into a serving dish and keep warm.

When the bread is cooked, remove it from the oven and allow it to cool in the tin for 5 minutes before turning it out. Cut the bread into thick chunks and serve warm with the dip.

## CORN BREAD PIZZAS

Use any left-over chilli corn bread and dip to make these small pizzas. Serve with a simple green salad.

*Chilli corn bread (see above recipe)*
*Mexican dip (see above recipe)*
*Salami or spicy sausage*
*Sliced tomatoes*
*Grated Edam cheese*

Slice the bread and lightly toast on one side under the grill. Spoon some dip on to the untoasted side and top with salami or sausage, tomatoes and cheese. Return to the grill and cook for 4–5 minutes or until bubbling hot.

# NEW POTATO AND BEETROOT SKEWERS
## *with grainy mustard sauce*

---

You don't have to use skewers for this recipe – simply combine dressing with vegetables and serve as a salad.

### SERVES 4
*2 lb (1 kg) unpeeled tiny new potatoes, scrubbed*
*1 lb (450 g) cooked baby beetroot*
*2 tablespoons sesame seeds*
*2 tablespoons sunflower oil*
*2 tablespoons lemon juice*
*Freshly ground black pepper*
*1 bunch watercress or lettuce leaves, washed and dried, to garnish*
### FOR THE GRAINY MUSTARD SAUCE
*2 tablespoons orange juice*
*2 tablespoons wholegrain mustard*
*2 oz (50 g) low-fat cream cheese*
*5 fl oz (150 ml) natural yoghurt*
*1 tablespoon soy sauce*
*Freshly ground black pepper*

Lightly grease a baking-tray.

Cut the potatoes in half and cut the cooked beetroot to the same size. Parboil the potatoes until just tender, drain and allow to cool.

Pre-heat the grill.

Mix together all the sauce ingredients, put into a serving dish and set to one side.

Thread the vegetables on to 4 skewers and place on the baking-tray. In a bowl, mix together the sesame seeds, oil and lemon juice and season well. Spoon and brush this mixture over the skewers and place under the grill for about 5 minutes, turning occasionally.

To serve, place the skewers on individual plates and garnish with the lettuce or watercress. Hand the sauce separately.

# SUMMER SATAY

---

If peanuts aren't your thing, try one of the dressings from pp. 121–123.

## SERVES 4
### FOR THE CRUDITÉS
*8 oz (225 g) broccoli, divided into florets*
*1 small cauliflower, divided into florets*
*1 lb (450 g) large carrots*
*1 cucumber, cut into thick chip-like sticks*
*4 oz (100 g) mushrooms or 1 bunch radishes*
*1 punnet mustard and cress*
### FOR THE SATAY SAUCE
*1 large onion, peeled and finely chopped or grated*
*3 tablespoons soy sauce*
*2 tablespoons water*
*1 clove garlic, peeled and crushed*
*1 teaspoon ground cumin*
*2 teaspoons chilli sauce*
*2 tablespoons crunchy peanut butter*
*Freshly ground black pepper*

Wash and prepare the vegetables and arrange on a large platter.

In a covered medium saucepan, simmer the onion in the soy sauce and water for 3–4 minutes or until well softened. Remove the lid and stir in the garlic, cumin, chilli sauce and peanut butter, and season with black pepper. Gradually add enough water, mixing all the time, to achieve a saucy consistency. Bring to the boil and pour into a heated shallow serving bowl.

Serve with the vegetables ready for dipping.

Alternatively, you could make this into a fondue feast. Fondues are easy to prepare and great fun to eat. Don't worry if you haven't got a fondue set – you can easily set up your own. As well as the medium saucepan in which to make the sauce, and forks for dipping, you will need a roasting-tin with four nightlights burning in it to supply the heat, and a wire rack on which to place the saucepan to keep hot at the table.

Give each of your guests an ordinary fork or a fondue fork. This will enable them to dip the vegetables into the tasty peanut sauce. Warm crusty bread, ham and tiny new potatoes are also interesting for dipping into fondues.

# OMELETTE FLORENTINE

This fluffy omelette is topped with a delicious combination of spinach and tomatoes. Serve it with warm wholemeal toast.

SERVES 4
1 tablespoon sunflower oil
1 large onion, peeled and sliced
4 oz (100 g) spinach, washed and finely chopped
1 teaspoon freshly grated nutmeg
Freshly ground black pepper
4 eggs
2 tablespoons water
1 tablespoon dried wholemeal breadcrumbs
12 oz (350 g) large tomatoes
FOR THE DRESSING
1 teaspoon French mustard
1 tablespoon lemon juice
2 tablespoons sunflower oil
1 clove garlic, peeled and crushed
1 teaspoon dried oregano

Pre-heat the grill.

In a large frying-pan, heat the oil and fry the onion until soft and golden-brown. Add the spinach and season well with nutmeg and black pepper. Toss over a fierce heat to evaporate any excess water.

In a bowl, beat the eggs together with 2 tablespoons of water and season well. Pour the mixture into the frying-pan and allow the omelette to set over a medium heat and turn golden-brown on the underside. Sprinkle with the breadcrumbs. Place the omelette under the grill and cook until just firm on top.

Combine all the dressing ingredients together.

Remove the omelette from the grill, lay over it the tomato slices and spoon over the dressing. Return the omelette to the grill and cook for a further 1–2 minutes or until the tomatoes begin to sizzle. Cut the omelette into wedges, take to the table in the pan and serve at once.

# OMELETTE SALAD

If you have any omelette left over from the previous recipe, try this super salad. Crusty brown rolls or granary toast go well with it.

### SERVES 3–4
*Cooked omelette (see above recipe)*
*Cucumber dressing (see p. 121)*
*8 oz (225 g) broad beans*
*1 Cos lettuce, washed and dried*

Cut the omelette into finger-length strips. Prepare the cucumber dressing (see p. 121). Cook the broad beans in boiling water until just tender, drain and refresh under cold running water. Tear the lettuce leaves into bite-size pieces and place in a large salad bowl. Toss in the broad beans and cold omelette strips. Drizzle over a little of the dressing and serve the rest separately.

# MAIN COURSES

## CHICKEN GADO GADO

## SPICY SPINACH AND LENTILS WITH ONION AND MINT RAITA AND NUTTY NAN

## MUSHROOM AND PIMENTO GALETTE WITH COS AND CARROT CRUNCH

## FISH SOUFFLÉ WITH WATERCRESS SAUCE AND HOT NEW POTATO AND CUCUMBER SALAD

## MARROW WITH CRACKED WHEAT AND GREEN BEANS WITH GARLIC

## CHICKEN GADO GADO

Try this unusual way of preparing chicken, but make sure you've got a sharp knife to cut the corn. Serve with lots of warm crusty granary bread to mop up the juices.

### SERVES 4
*1 tablespoon sunflower oil*
*4 chicken thighs, boned and skinned*
*1 tablespoon desiccated coconut*
*1 corn on the cob, thinly sliced and parboiled for 5 minutes*
*8 oz (225 g) runner beans, prepared and sliced*
*2 cloves garlic, peeled and crushed (optional)*
*5 fl oz (150 ml) vegetable or chicken stock*
*6 oz (175 g) green noodles*
*2 tablespoons crunchy peanut butter*
*5 fl oz (150 ml) orange juice*
*1 tablespoon soy sauce*
*4 tablespoons water*
*2 teaspoons chilli sauce*
*Freshly ground black pepper*
*Chopped parsley to garnish*

Heat the oil in a large frying-pan or wok and stir-fry the chicken for 5 minutes or until it browns slightly. Add the coconut and toss over the heat for a further minute. Reduce the heat and add the parboiled corn, beans, garlic (if using) and stock. Cover and simmer for 10 minutes or until the chicken is cooked right through. Add extra stock if necessary.

Plunge the noodles into boiling water and cook for 4 minutes or until tender. Drain well.

In a bowl, mix together the peanut butter, orange juice, soy sauce, water and chilli sauce. Pour this over the chicken and add the cooked noodles. Toss these together over the heat once more, cover and heat through for 2–3 minutes. Season to taste, scatter the top with chopped parsley and serve from the pan if possible.

## SPICY SPINACH AND LENTILS
### *with onion and mint raita and nutty nan*

If you haven't got time to make your own nan bread, serve the spicy spinach and lentils with warm pitta bread instead.

### SERVES 4
### *FOR THE SPICY SPINACH AND LENTILS*
*1 large onion, peeled and finely sliced*
*1 clove garlic, peeled and crushed*
*1 tablespoon mild curry paste*
*6 oz (175 g) red lentils*
*1 tablespoon tomato purée*
*1 pint (600 ml) vegetable stock*
*Freshly ground black pepper*
*1 lb (450 g) fresh spinach, well washed and roughly chopped*
### *FOR THE ONION AND MINT RAITA*
*1 medium onion, peeled and grated*
*10 fl oz (300 ml) natural yoghurt*
*1 teaspoon mint sauce*
*1 teaspoon dill seeds*
*Freshly ground black pepper*

## FOR THE NUTTY NAN
*½ sachet easy-blend yeast*
*Pinch of salt*
*8 oz (225 g) wholemeal flour*
*8 oz (225 g) plain flour*
*15 fl oz (450 ml) warm water*
*2 oz (50 g) sultanas*
*2 oz (50 g) ground almonds*
*Milk*
*Poppy seeds to decorate*

For the nan, combine the yeast, salt and flours in a large mixing bowl and mix well. Gradually pour in enough of the warm water to mix it to the consistency of a firm, moist paste. Knead the dough on a floured surface for 5 minutes. Place in a bowl, cover and leave in a warm place to rise for 40 minutes.

Meanwhile, for the spicy spinach and lentils, dry-fry the onion and garlic in the curry paste in a large saucepan until softened. Add the lentils, tomato purée and vegetable stock. Season well. Bring to the boil, reduce the heat and simmer, covered, for 20 minutes or until the lentils are soft.

Combine the raita ingredients in a bowl.

Pre-heat the oven to gas mark 6, 400°F (200°C). Lightly grease 2 baking-trays.

Turn the risen nan dough out on to a floured surface and knead in the sultanas and ground almonds. Divide it into 6 equal portions and roll and pat each one into a flat round or oval. Place the nans on the prepared baking-trays, brush with milk and scatter with poppy seeds. Bake in the oven for 10-15 minutes.

Add the chopped spinach to the cooked lentils, cover and cook for a further 6–7 minutes or until the spinach is tender. Check the seasoning and adjust as necessary, then transfer to a serving dish. Serve with the raita and warm nan.

# MUSHROOM AND PIMENTO GALETTE
## *with Cos and carrot crunch*

---

This round, open pie makes the most of mushrooms, which have the added bonus of being available all year round. The big flat ones have the best flavour.

The galette freezes well. If you are cooking for only one or two people, make the whole galette and, when it is cool, cut it into quarters, wrap and freeze. Take it out of the freezer when needed and simply re-heat from frozen. Serve warm with salad.

**SERVES 4**

*FOR THE BASE*

*8 oz (225 g) granary flour*

*4 oz (100 g) self-raising flour*

*2 tablespoons sunflower oil*

*Warm water to mix*

*FOR THE FILLING*

*1 × 14 oz (400 g) tin chopped tomatoes*

*1 clove garlic, peeled and crushed*

*1 tablespoon tomato purée*

*1 onion, peeled and sliced*

*8 oz (225 g) large flat mushrooms, wiped and sliced*

*1 large red pepper, de-seeded and sliced*

*2 tablespoons sunflower seeds*

*4 oz (100 g) white Cheshire cheese, crumbled*

*2 teaspoons dried sage*

*Freshly ground black pepper*

*Chopped parsley*

*FOR THE COS AND CARROT CRUNCH*

*1 Cos lettuce*

*2 carrots, peeled and grated*

*1 tablespoon lemon juice*

*Freshly ground black pepper*

Pre-heat the oven to gas mark 6, 400°F (200°C). Generously flour a large baking-tray.

To make the base, combine the flours in a large mixing bowl. Make a well in the centre and pour in the sunflower oil. Gradually add enough warm water to mix to a firm but moist dough.

On the floured baking-tray, roll out the dough into a 12-inch (30-cm) circle. Neaten the edges and form a slightly raised border around the edge with your fingers. Prick the base with a fork and bake in the oven for 10 minutes.

For the filling, simmer the tomatoes, garlic, tomato purée and sliced onion together in a saucepan for 8 minutes or until thickened and reduced by half. Remove the base from the oven and spread the tomato sauce evenly over the top. Scatter with the sliced mushrooms, red pepper, sunflower seeds, cheese and dried sage. Return the galette to the oven and bake for a further 15–20 minutes or until golden-brown and bubbling hot.

Wash and dry the lettuce, place it in a salad bowl and toss well with grated carrots, lemon juice and black pepper.

Remove the galette from the oven, grind over some black pepper to taste, scatter with chopped parsley and serve at once.

# FISH SOUFFLÉ
## *with watercress sauce and hot new potato and cucumber salad*

A foolproof soufflé to impress your friends.

### SERVES 4
### *FOR THE FISH SOUFFLÉ*
*1 × 7 oz (200 g) tin pink salmon*
*½ oz (15 g) margarine*
*1 tablespoon plain flour*
*1 level tablespoon paprika*
*10 fl oz (300 ml) semi-skimmed milk*
*4 eggs, separated*
*Freshly ground black pepper*
### *FOR THE WATERCRESS SAUCE*
*8 oz (225 g) fromage frais*
*1 bunch watercress, washed, dried and chopped*
*1 teaspoon French mustard*
*Freshly ground black pepper*

## FOR THE HOT NEW POTATO AND CUCUMBER SALAD

1½ lb (750 g) unpeeled new potatoes, scrubbed
2 tablespoons sunflower oil
1 teaspoon runny honey
Freshly ground black pepper
1 tablespoon lemon juice
2 teaspoons French mustard
½ cucumber, cut into chip-like sticks

Pre-heat the oven to gas mark 6, 400°F (200°C). Lightly grease a 2-pint (1.2-litre) soufflé or ovenproof dish.

Drain the salmon, reserving the liquid, and flake the fish. Melt the margarine for the soufflé in a small saucepan and stir in the flour and paprika. Cook for 1 minute and remove from the heat. Pour in the milk and reserved salmon liquid and blend well until smooth. Return the pan to the heat, bring to the boil and simmer for 3 minutes, stirring occasionally. Set the sauce to one side to cool.

In a large, dry mixing bowl, beat the egg whites until stiff.

Add the fish and the egg yolks to the cooled sauce, season with black pepper and turn into a large mixing bowl. Using a large metal spoon, fold in half the whisked egg whites quite quickly. Add the remaining egg whites and fold in very gently. Spoon this mixture into the prepared soufflé dish. Bake in the oven for 20–25 minutes or until risen, firm and golden-brown.

Meanwhile, cook the potatoes in boiling water until just tender. In a small bowl, combine the dressing ingredients for the potato salad – oil, honey, black pepper, lemon juice and mustard.

Liquidise the watercress sauce ingredients together and season to taste.

When they are cooked, drain the potatoes and return to the saucepan. Add the cucumber and pour in the dressing. Toss over a high heat until glazed and season well. Turn into a serving dish.

Remove the soufflé from the oven and, using two large spoons, make a parting in the centre and pour in half of the sauce. Serve at once, accompanied by the potato salad and the rest of the sauce.

# MARROW WITH CRACKED WHEAT
## and green beans with garlic

Marrows are cheap and plentiful in the summer. Here's a recipe combining marrow with cracked wheat and dill.

SERVES 4
*FOR THE MARROW WITH CRACKED WHEAT*
*8 oz (225 g) cracked wheat*
*1 tablespoon sunflower oil*
*1 large onion, peeled and chopped*
*2 lb (1 kg) marrow*
*2 teaspoons dill seeds*
*¼ teaspoon freshly grated nutmeg*
*4 oz (100 g) raisins*
*1 bay leaf*
*1 pint (600 ml) vegetable stock*
*Freshly ground black pepper*
*2 large carrots, scrubbed and grated*
*2 oz (50 g) flaked almonds, toasted*
*1 lemon, cut into wedges*
*FOR THE GREEN BEANS WITH GARLIC*
*1 lb (450 g) runner beans, prepared and sliced*
*1 tablespoon sunflower oil*
*2 large tomatoes, chopped*
*1 large clove garlic, peeled and crushed*
*Freshly ground black pepper*

Soak the cracked wheat in cold water for 20 minutes.

Heat the oil in a large frying-pan or wok and cook the onion until softened. Peel the marrow and cut it in half. Remove the seeds and cut the flesh into large bite-size pieces. Add the marrow to the pan, along with the dill seeds and nutmeg and gently fry for 2–3 minutes. Stir in the raisins and bay leaf and pour on the stock. Season well. Cover, reduce the heat and simmer for 15 minutes, adding extra liquid if needed. At the end of this time, drain the cracked wheat and add it to the pan. Cook for a further 8–10 minutes.

Plunge the runner beans into a saucepan of boiling water and cook for

5–6 minutes or until just tender. Meanwhile, in a mixing bowl, combine the oil, tomatoes and garlic and season well. Drain the runner beans and return them to the saucepan over a medium heat. Stir in the tomato and garlic mixture and toss over the heat. Turn this into a heated serving dish and keep warm.

Remove the lid from the marrow and fork in the carrots and flaked almonds. Spoon into a large serving dish and surround with lemon wedges.

## STUFFED CUP MUSHROOMS

Try these tasty stuffed mushrooms if you have any marrow with cracked wheat left over from the previous recipe.

*Large cup mushrooms*
*Sunflower oil*
*Freshly ground black pepper*
*Marrow with cracked wheat mixture (see above recipe)*
*Grated Cheddar cheese*
*Chopped parsley*

Pre-heat the oven to gas mark 6, 400°F (200°C).

Remove the stalks from the mushrooms and wipe the tops with damp kitchen paper. Place the tops upside down on a baking-tray, drizzle over a little sunflower oil and season well. Spoon the marrow with cracked wheat mixture into the cups. Sprinkle with a little grated cheese and chopped parsley. Bake in the oven for 12–15 minutes and finish off under the grill, if needed, until golden-brown.

# PUDDINGS

SUMMER RED FRUITS WITH A MAIZE CRUST

GOOSEBERRY FOOL

PEACH GRATIN

RED FRUIT SALAD WITH EXOTIC SAUCE

QUICK STRAWBERRY ICE

SPICED NECTARINES

SQUASHY RHUBARB CAKE

GOOSEBERRY AND RAISIN PUDDING

## SUMMER RED FRUITS
### *with a maize crust*

Maize crust gives a crisp biscuit top to this pungent fruit pie.

### SERVES 4
$1\frac{1}{2}$ lb (750 g) assorted red fruits (strawberries, plums, raspberries, redcurrants, etc.), washed and trimmed
Juice and grated rind of 1 orange
1 bay leaf
4 oz (100 g) salted margarine
1 large egg
4 oz (100 g) maize flour or semolina
4 oz (100 g) rice flour
Ground cinnamon
Caster sugar
Fromage frais to serve

Lightly grease a 10-inch (25-cm) flan dish. Pre-heat the oven to gas mark 6, 400°F (200°C).

Place the prepared fruits in the flan dish. Pour over the juice of the orange and put the bay leaf on top.

In a mixing bowl, beat together the margarine and grated orange rind until soft. Carefully mix in the egg, maize flour (or semolina) and rice flour and bind together to form a paste. Roll out the paste, using the cinnamon and caster sugar to prevent sticking. Lay this over the fruits and bake in the oven for 15–20 minutes. Serve straight from the flan dish with lots of fromage frais.

# GOOSEBERRY FOOL

SERVES 4
*1 lb (450 g) gooseberries*
*3 tablespoons water*
*2 oz (50 g) brown sugar or to taste*
*8 oz (225 g) low-fat fromage frais*

Make the most of gooseberries in the summer: their season is short. Try this simple fool recipe. Stew the gooseberries with a little water and sugar, allow to cool, then mash them lightly. Fold in low-fat fromage frais, spoon into glasses and chill before serving. Alternatively, freeze the mixture for a sharp, tangy ice-cream.

# PEACH GRATIN

Try this mouth-watering method of cooking peaches Italian style.

SERVES 4
*4 ripe peaches*
*4 oz (100 g) blackberries*
*5 fl oz (150 ml) natural yoghurt*
*Juice and grated rind of 1 orange*
*2 tablespoons demerara sugar*

Pre-heat the grill. Lightly grease an ovenproof dish.

Cut the peaches in half and remove the stones. Lay the peach halves, cut side up, in the prepared dish. Scatter over the berries.

In a mixing bowl, combine the yoghurt with the orange juice and rind. Pour evenly over the peaches and scatter with the sugar. Place under the grill for 4–5 minutes or until golden-brown and bubbling hot.

# RED FRUIT SALAD
## *with exotic sauce*

---

Serve with oatcakes or muesli-style biscuits.

### SERVES 4–8
*¼ watermelon, peeled, de-seeded and diced*
*4 oz (100 g) black cherries, stoned; or black grapes*
*8 oz (225 g) strawberries, hulled and halved*
*10 fl oz (300 ml) orange juice*
*2 teaspoons runny honey*
*1 teaspoon ground allspice*
*1 bay leaf*
*2 sprigs mint, chopped*

Prepare the fruit, place in a large bowl and chill in the refrigerator.

In a saucepan, simmer the orange juice, honey, allspice and bay leaf together for 8 minutes. Pour the hot syrup over the chilled fruit and, having allowed to cool, chill again.

Before serving, stir in the chopped mint.

# QUICK STRAWBERRY ICE

---

A simple way of making any summer fruit ice-cream. Remember to remove it from the freezer at least 20–30 minutes before serving.

### SERVES 4
*1 lb (450 g) fresh strawberries, hulled and halved; or other seasonal soft fruit*
*2 tablespoons runny honey*
*4 oz (100 g) fromage frais*

Place the strawberries in the freezer until half-frozen. Put them in a liquidiser, spoon over the honey and liquidise until smooth. Turn into a mixing bowl and gently fold in the fromage frais to achieve a marbled effect. Return to the freezer for at least 3–4 hours, until needed.

# SPICED NECTARINES

Fromage frais and muesli-style biscuits are a nice accompaniment – or how about trying some spiced cream (see p. 125).

SERVES 4
*4 nectarines*
*FOR THE SYRUP*
*1 tablespoon runny honey*
*10 fl oz (300 ml) orange juice*
*1 bay leaf*
*1 stick cinnamon or ½ teaspoon ground cinnamon*
*A handful of coriander seeds, crushed*

In a saucepan and over a medium heat, blend the syrup ingredients together. Bring to the boil, reduce the heat and simmer for 5 minutes or until the syrup starts to feel slightly sticky.

Wash the nectarines and prick all over with the point of a knife. Place in the syrup, cover and cook gently for 30 minutes or until tender. Serve hot or allow to cool in the syrup and chill well before serving.

# SQUASHY RHUBARB CAKE

Try this thinly sliced, served with fruit sorbet or ice-cream.

SERVES 4
*8 oz (225 g) wholemeal flour*
*2 teaspoons baking powder*
*2 teaspoons ground cinnamon*
*3 tablespoons runny honey*
*8 oz (225 g) raisins*
*2 eggs*
*5 fl oz (150 ml) semi-skimmed milk*
*8 oz (225 g) rhubarb, chopped into small pieces*
*2 tablespoons grapenuts or muesli*
*Icing sugar for dusting*

Pre-heat the oven to gas mark 4, 350°F (180°C). Lightly grease and flour an 8-inch (20-cm) deep-sided cake tin or a 1 lb (450-g) loaf tin.

In a large mixing bowl, blend the flour, baking powder and cinnamon. Add the honey, raisins, eggs and milk and beat well. Fold in the rhubarb. Spoon the mixture into the prepared tin and sprinkle with the grapenuts or muesli. Bake for 50 minutes or until the cake is firm and springy. When cooked, allow to cool in the tin for 10 minutes, then turn out and finish cooling on a wire rack. Dust with the icing sugar and serve.

# GOOSEBERRY AND RAISIN PUDDING

To show this pudding off at its best, you need to turn it out. Go on – be brave! Tinned gooseberries may be used instead of fresh ones: just omit the water from the recipe. The pudding can be served warm with fromage frais, though it's just as good cold. It's also great as a teatime cake.

### SERVES 4
*1 lb (450 g) fresh gooseberries, washed and prepared*
*4 oz (100 g) raisins*
*4 tablespoons orange juice*
*4 tablespoons water*
*4 oz (100 g) sunflower margarine*
*4 oz (100 g) brown sugar*
*2 eggs*
*3 oz (75 g) self-raising wholemeal flour*
*3 oz (75 g) self-raising flour*

Pre-heat the oven to gas mark 5, 375°F (190°C). Lightly grease a 2-pint (1.2-litre) ovenproof dish.

Combine the gooseberries, raisins, orange juice and water in the prepared dish.

In a mixing bowl, beat the margarine and sugar together. Add the eggs gradually with a little flour, beating all the time. Fold in the remaining flour. Add a little water to obtain a dropping consistency. Spoon and spread the mixture over the fruit and bake in the oven for 40–45 minutes or until the pudding is golden and risen.

Cool slightly and serve from the dish; or turn on to a serving plate.

# BARBECUE SPECIALS

## TANGY BARBECUED CHICKEN
### *with garlic potatoes in foil, tomato and apple relish and 'simply spinach'*

---

Corn-on-the-cob barbecued in its leaves goes well with this – simply cook for 10–15 minutes, turning occasionally.

### SERVES 4
*FOR THE CHICKEN*
*10 fl oz (300 ml) beer or apple juice*
*3 cloves garlic, peeled and crushed*
*1 tablespoon wholegrain mustard*
*1 tablespoon coriander seeds, crushed or ground*
*1 sprig rosemary, sage or thyme, plus extra to garnish*
*1 bay leaf*
*1 tablespoon runny honey*
*4 chicken legs, whole or halved*
*FOR THE GARLIC POTATOES*
*1½ lb (750 g) unpeeled new potatoes, scrubbed and parboiled for 5 minutes*
*1 large onion, peeled and sliced*
*2 tablespoons sunflower oil*
*1 clove garlic, peeled and crushed*
*Freshly ground black pepper*
*Tomato and apple relish (see p. 116)*
*'Simply spinach' (see pp. 23–24)*

In a mixing bowl, prepare the chicken marinade: combine the beer or apple juice, garlic, mustard, coriander, herbs and honey. Add the chicken joints, coating them well. Allow to marinate for 2 hours, basting occasionally.

Prepare the relish (see p. 116) and salad (see pp. 23–24) and place in the refrigerator to keep fresh.

Prepare and light the barbecue. Prepare 4 double-thickness sheets of aluminium foil, lightly greased (the size will depend on the number of potatoes).

Parboil the potatoes for 5 minutes. Drain and divide between the foil sheets. Mix together the onion, sunflower oil and garlic and season with black pepper. Enclose the foil parcels tightly and barbecue for 45 minutes.

When the potatoes have been cooking for 10 minutes, place the chicken on the barbecue. Using the marinade for basting, cook the chicken for 30–35 minutes, turning occasionally until cooked through (no red or pink juices should appear when the flesh is pierced deeply with a skewer). Alternatively, if the weather lets you down, cook the chicken in the oven at gas mark 5, 375°F (190°C), for 40–45 minutes (in this case you could remove the skin, if you wished, for a lower-fat meal). Garnish the cooked chicken with additional fresh herbs if desired and then serve with the accompanying dishes.

# BANANAS FLAMED IN THEIR SKINS

If you are having a barbecue, make the most of it by using it to cook both your main course and your pudding.

SERVES 4
*4 large ripe bananas*
*8 oz (225 g) fromage frais*
*2 tablespoons runny honey*

Wash the bananas, trim off the ends and place them, still in their skins, on the barbecue (not the hottest part). Grill for about 6–8 minutes or until the skins have completely blackened, turning occasionally. Transfer the bananas to a serving dish and serve the fromage frais and honey in separate bowls. Allow your guests to open the banana skins and fill with fromage frais and pour on honey to taste.

Alternatively, you could wrap the bananas in aluminium foil to cook them, in which case allow a few extra minutes' cooking time on the barbecue.

# AUTUMN

Autumn, my favourite time of year, when apples, golden pumpkins and root vegetables come into their own.

As the evenings get longer and the temperature drops, there are plenty of dishes to keep out the first winter's chill. Rabbit is in season and makes a delicious change from chicken, but if you cannot buy it fresh from your butcher, look for frozen rabbit which has been portioned and prepared in the supermarkets.

Root and tuber vegetables including potatoes, sweet potatoes, parsnips, turnips and swedes make a colourful comeback in the autumn. These tasty, sweet vegetables are versatile, cheap and form the basis of autumn stews, pies, gratins and soufflés. They can also be puréed and combined together to make delicious, creamy vegetable toppings or thick soups. Cabbage is cheap at this time of year, too, so just steam or boil it; try it sliced thickly and stir-fried in soy sauce, garlic and black pepper.

Make the most of autumn hedgerow fruits like blackberries, wild damsons and elderberries. Many of the pudding recipes can be adapted to use these fruits if you can find them.

# AUTUMN SPECIALS

Baked potatoes are the traditional food for chilly nights especially for Hallowe'en and Guy Fawkes' parties. Try the special menu for children's parties or for simple, cosy suppers for family and friends to eat indoors or around the bonfire.

## HALLOWE'EN SUPPER SPECIALS
### WITCHES' WINTER CAULDRON (p. 83)

### CRACKWHEAT MEATLOAF WITH DEVILLED PIMENTO SAUCE AND ROASTED ROOT VEGETABLES (pp. 83–84)

## GUY FAWKES' SUPPER SPECIAL
### BAKED POTATOES MELODY (p. 85)

## SEASONAL VEGETABLES

| | | |
|---|---|---|
| Cabbage/greens | Leeks | Runner beans |
| Carrots | Mushrooms | Spinach |
| Cauliflower | Onions | Swede |
| Celery | Parsnips | Sweetcorn |
| Courgettes | Pumpkin | Tomatoes |

## SEASONAL FRUITS

| | | |
|---|---|---|
| Apples | Dates | Peaches |
| Blackberries | Grapes | Pears |
| Blueberries | Greengages | Plums |
| Damsons | | |

## SEASONAL FISH

| | | |
|---|---|---|
| Mussels | Sprats | Whiting |

## SEASONAL MEAT

Rabbit

# LIGHT SUPPERS AND LUNCHES

POTATO PLOUGHMAN'S

SURPRISE POP-OVERS WITH CARROT AND
COURGETTE SALAD

MUSSEL SOUP WITH GARLIC SAUCE

GREEN SOUP WITH CUCUMBER NOODLES

BAKED PEAR AND CHEESE STRUDELS

PUMPKIN AND BLUE CHEESE RISOTTO

SAVOURY PUMPKIN AND NUTMEG TART

GREEN CAULIFLOWER GRATIN

## POTATO PLOUGHMAN'S

Here's my version of a ploughman's lunch.

SERVES 4
*1 lb (450 g) eating apples*
*2 teaspoons honey*
*1 lb (450 g) unpeeled potatoes, washed, halved and parboiled for 5 minutes*
*1 small onion, peeled and grated*
*1 oz (25 g) porridge oats*
*1 large egg*
*Freshly ground black pepper*
*1 tablespoon sunflower oil*
*6 oz (175 g) Edam cheese, cut into 4 pieces*

Wash, core and slice the apples. Place them in a saucepan with the honey
and a little cold water. Cover and cook gently until soft.

Grate the parboiled potatoes and combine with the onion, oats and egg in a bowl. Season well. Heat the oil in a frying-pan and drop tablespoons of the mixture into the pan (you may need to spread the mixture out a little). Cook the potato cakes for 4–5 minutes on each side or until golden and cooked through. Drain on kitchen paper.

Divide the hot potato cakes between 4 dinner plates, each with a hunk of Edam cheese and a generous spoonful of warm apple sauce. Serve at once.

## TOMATO-TOPPED POTATO CAKES

Left-over potato cakes can be used to make this simple, quick lunch or supper dish. Place them on a grill rack, top with sliced tomatoes, scatter with some dried herbs and a little grated cheese and pop under the grill until heated through and golden-brown. Serve with a green salad.

# SURPRISE POP-OVERS
## *with carrot and courgette salad*

A fun and tasty way of presenting a vegetable salad.

### SERVES 4
*4 wholemeal or granary baps or rolls*
*1 clove garlic, peeled and crushed*
*2 tablespoons sunflower oil*
### FOR THE CARROT AND COURGETTE SALAD
*4 large carrots, peeled*
*2 large courgettes*
*Zingy dressing (see p. 122)*
*2 teaspoons poppy seeds*
*Freshly ground black pepper*

Pre-heat the oven to gas mark 6, 400°F (200°C).

Cut the tops from the baps or rolls and reserve. Scoop out the insides – keep these in the freezer for when you need breadcrumbs. In a small cup, mix together the garlic and sunflower oil. Using a pastry brush, brush the tops and insides of the baps with the oil and garlic. Place the baps on a baking-tray and bake for 8–10 minutes or until crisp.

Meanwhile prepare the salad. Using a potato peeler, strip the carrots and courgettes into ribbons. Toss the vegetables in the dressing, add the poppy seeds and season well. Remove the baps from the oven and fill with the salad. Replace the lids and serve at once.

# MUSSEL SOUP
## *with garlic sauce*

This is the start of the mussel season – and they are not as expensive as you might think. Serve your soup rustic-style: take the steaming pan to the table where ladle, crusty bread and garlic sauce are waiting.

### SERVES 4
*2 leeks, washed and shredded*
*1 tablespoon sunflower oil*
*4 large tomatoes, chopped*
*1 tablespoon plain flour*
*2 pints (1.2 litres) vegetable stock*
*1 × 14 oz (400 g) tin chopped tomatoes with herbs*
*1 bay leaf*
*Freshly ground black pepper*
*2 lb (1 kg) fresh mussels*
*1 loaf crusty granary bread, thickly sliced*
*Chopped parsley to garnish*
*FOR THE GARLIC SAUCE*
*3 tablespoons fromage frais*
*2 cloves garlic, peeled and crushed*
*1 tablespoon tomato purée*
*2 teaspoons Tabasco sauce*
*1 tablespoon chopped parsley*

In a large saucepan, fry the leeks in the oil until they are golden. Add the fresh tomatoes and flour and cook for 1 minute. Pour in the stock and tinned tomatoes. Put in the bay leaf, season well, bring to the boil and simmer for 35–40 minutes.

Meanwhile, soak the mussels in cold water and scrub them well. Remove any threads and throw away any mussels which are cracked or which remain open when tapped.

In a small bowl, mix together the garlic sauce ingredients and season to taste. Spoon into a small serving dish.

Add the mussels to the soup and cover. Simmer for a further 5 minutes or until the mussels have completely opened. Discard any which fail to open.

Lightly toast the bread under the grill. Scatter the soup with chopped parsley and serve. The garlic sauce should be spread on the toast and eaten with the soup.

# GREEN SOUP
## with cucumber noodles

An attractive way of presenting a simple pea soup using hot cucumber noodles.

### SERVES 4
*8 oz (225 g) dried green split peas, well washed*
*2 teaspoons curry powder*
*1 large onion, peeled and chopped*
*4 sticks celery, washed and chopped*
*3 pints (1.75 litres) vegetable stock*
*1 bay leaf*
*1 cucumber*
*Freshly ground black pepper*
*Juice of 1 orange*

In a large saucepan, dry-fry the split peas, curry powder, onion and celery for 2–3 minutes. Add the stock and bay leaf. Bring to the boil and remove any scum which may come to the surface. Cover and simmer gently for 1½ hours, or until the peas are very soft.

Cut the cucumber in half. Slice each half lengthways into slices and then each slice into thin strips to resemble noodles. Plunge the cucumber noodles into boiling water for 1 minute, drain and refresh under cold water.

Liquidise half the soup and mix it with the rest to obtain a coarse texture. Season well and add the orange juice. Ladle the soup into bowls and scatter in the cucumber noodles. Grind over plenty of black pepper and serve piping hot.

# BAKED PEAR AND CHEESE STRUDELS

These delicious warm pear and cheese parcels, served with a crisp salad, will certainly tickle your taste buds.

SERVES 4
*½ tablespoon sunflower oil*
*1 medium onion, peeled and chopped*
*2 large pears, cored and sliced*
*8 oz (225 g) ready-made puff or shortcrust pastry*
*4 oz (100 g) Cheddar cheese, grated*
*Freshly ground black pepper*
*Freshly grated nutmeg*
*Milk to glaze*
FOR THE SALAD
*1 round lettuce*
*1 punnet mustard and cress, washed and dried*
*1 bunch radishes, washed and sliced*
FOR THE OPTIONAL SALAD DRESSING
*2 teaspoons poppy seeds*
*1 tablespoon white wine vinegar*
*1 teaspoon mustard*
*3 tablespoons sunflower oil*

In a frying-pan, heat the oil and gently fry the onion for 2–3 minutes. Add the sliced pears and toss over a fierce heat for a further 2 minutes. Remove the pan from the heat and set to one side to cool.

Pre-heat the oven to gas mark 6, 400°F (200°C). Lightly grease a baking-tray.

On a floured surface, roll out the pastry into a large square and divide into quarters. Add the cheese to the cooled pears and season the mixture with black pepper and nutmeg. Spoon equal amounts of the mixture on to the middle of each piece of pastry. Brush the edges of the squares with milk and draw the edges together, pressing to seal them and form pyramid-shaped parcels. Place the parcels on the baking-tray and brush with a little milk. Bake in the oven for 15–20 minutes or until crisp and golden-brown.

Meanwhile, wash and prepare the salad ingredients and toss in the dressing (if using). Divide between 4 large plates. Remove the baked strudels from the oven and place one on each plate with the salad. Serve at once.

# PUMPKIN AND BLUE CHEESE RISOTTO

There's plenty of pumpkin about in the autumn, it's cheap and gives a lovely creamy texture to this risotto. Great for a Guy Fawkes supper party.

## SERVES 6–8 AS A STARTER OR 4 AS A MAIN COURSE
*1 lb (450 g) pumpkin*
*1 tablespoon sunflower oil*
*1 medium onion, peeled and chopped*
*1 clove garlic, peeled and crushed*
*12 oz (350 g) Italian easy-cook brown rice*
*1 bay leaf*
*1½ pints (900 ml) vegetable stock*
*5 fl oz (150 ml) apple juice*
*4 oz (100 g) blue cheese, crumbled*
*2 tablespoons chopped parsley*
*1 tablespoon pumpkin seeds, toasted*

Remove the rind from the pumpkin and cut the flesh into bite-size pieces. In a large frying-pan or wok, heat the oil and cook the onion and garlic until soft. Add the rice, pumpkin and bay leaf and cook for 30 seconds over a high heat. Pour on the stock and apple juice, reduce the heat and simmer gently until the liquid has almost been absorbed. Do not let the risotto dry out – add a little water if necessary. You should be left with 5 fl oz (150 ml) liquid in the pan, with the rice cooked and creamy and the pumpkin tender.

At the last minute, fork in the crumbled blue cheese and chopped parsley. Serve sprinkled with the pumpkin seeds – straight from the pan or after transferring to a heated serving dish.

Left-over risotto can become rather stodgy when re-heated. Instead, try it cold, served with a plain green salad tossed in a dressing of your choice (see pp. 121–123).

# SAVOURY PUMPKIN AND NUTMEG TART

Pumpkin has a similar texture to marrow and is available throughout the autumn months. Treat it like potato: it can be roasted, boiled, baked, stewed and puréed and goes well in pies and tarts.

### SERVES 4

*2 lb (1 kg) pumpkin flesh, cut into 2-inch (5-cm) pieces*
*2 tablespoons sunflower oil*
*2 tablespoons soy sauce*
*Freshly ground black pepper*
*8 oz (225 g) ready-made shortcrust pastry*
*1 teaspoon freshly grated nutmeg*
*1 egg*
*4 tablespoons fromage frais*
*4 tablespoons dried wholemeal breadcrumbs*
*2 tablespoons pumpkin seeds, toasted*

Pre-heat the oven to gas mark 6, 400°F (200°C). Lightly grease an 8-inch (20-cm) flan tin.

Place the pumpkin in a roasting-tin and pour over it the oil and soy sauce. Season well and bake in the oven for 20–25 minutes or until softened.

Roll out the pastry on a floured surface and line the prepared tin. Allow to 'relax' in the refrigerator for 15 minutes. Bake the flan case 'blind' in the oven for 20–25 minutes or until crisp (see p. 28).

Place the roasted pumpkin in the cooked flan case and season with nutmeg. In a bowl, beat together the egg and fromage frais and pour this over the pumpkin. Scatter with the breadcrumbs and bake in the oven for a further 20–25 minutes. Sprinkle over the toasted pumpkin seeds and serve at once.

# GREEN CAULIFLOWER GRATIN

Fed up with cauliflower cheese? Try this dish as a tasty lunch or supper dish with warm, crusty, wholemeal rolls or as a vegetable accompaniment to a main course.

SERVES 4

*8 oz (225 g) frozen peas*
*8 fl oz (250 ml) vegetable stock*
*1 bay leaf*
*1 large cauliflower, divided into florets*
*2 oz (50 g) flaked almonds*
*2 oz (50 g) Cheddar cheese, grated*
*1 tablespoon dried wholemeal breadcrumbs*

In a saucepan, simmer the peas, stock and bay leaf together for 15 minutes.

Plunge the cauliflower florets into boiling water and cook until just tender. Drain and refresh under cold water.

Remove the bay leaf from the peas and liquidise the mixture until very smooth and thick. Season well.

Pre-heat the grill.

Arrange the cauliflower florets in a shallow ovenproof dish. Mix together the almonds, cheese and breadcrumbs. Spoon the green pea sauce over the cauliflower and scatter the almond and breadcrumb mixture on top. Place this under the grill for 4–5 minutes or until bubbling hot and golden-brown. Serve at once.

## *CAULIFLOWER AND PEA SOUP*

Put left-overs from the above recipe in a saucepan and barely cover with vegetable stock. Bring to the boil and simmer for 3–4 minutes. Place in a liquidiser and blend until smooth. Return to the saucepan and check the consistency, adding extra stock if the soup is too thick. Season to taste and keep warm.

Meanwhile, plunge some pasta into boiling water and cook until *al dente* (slightly firm to the bite). Ladle the soup into large soup bowls. Drain the pasta, season well and spoon into the soup. Finish off with a sprinkling of grated cheese and black pepper.

# MAIN COURSES

FISH PIE WITH PEAS

GREEN LENTIL CASSOULET WITH 'EVERYTHING GREEN' SALAD

RABBIT WITH PRUNES SERVED WITH POTATO AND PARSNIP PURÉE

MUSHROOM AND RUNNER BEAN CLAFOUTIS WITH MUSTARD POTATOES AND FRESH TOMATO RELISH

SPICED CHICKEN WITH POTATOES IN COCONUT

BARLEY POT WITH BROCCOLI IN TASTY TOMATO SAUCE

## FISH PIE
*with peas*

SERVES 4
*FOR THE FISH PIE*
*12 oz (350 g) whiting*
*1¼ pints (750 ml) semi-skimmed milk*
*2 oz (50 g) butter*
*2 oz (50 g) plain flour*
*½ teaspoon freshly grated nutmeg*
*Freshly ground black pepper*
*3 eggs, hard-boiled and chopped*
*8 oz (225 g) carrots, scrubbed and grated*
*2 tablespoons chopped parsley*
*2 lb (1 kg) floury potatoes, peeled and cut into even-sized pieces*
*2 teaspoons turmeric*
*FOR THE PEAS*
*1 lb (450 g) frozen peas*
*Knob of butter*
*Freshly ground black pepper*

Pre-heat the oven to gas mark 5, 375°F (190°C).

Place the fish, skin side up, in a roasting-tin. Pour over 1 pint (600 ml) of the milk and bake in the oven for 10–15 minutes or until the skin peels away easily from the fish. Using a fish slice, remove the cooked fish from the milk and place it on a plate. Reserve the milk.

In a small saucepan, melt the butter and add the flour and nutmeg and cook for 1 minute. Remove from the heat and add all the reserved milk in which the fish was cooked, stirring well until the mixture is smooth. Return the pan to the heat and bring to the boil. Simmer for 3–4 minutes and season well.

Carefully skin the fish and, using two forks, flake the flesh into pieces. Add the fish, chopped eggs, grated carrots and parsley to the sauce and season again to taste. Pile the mixture into an ovenproof dish and set to one side.

Increase the oven temperature to gas mark 6, 400°F (200°C).

Cook the potatoes in boiling water until just tender. Drain and mash thoroughly with the turmeric. Beat in the remaining 5 fl oz (150 ml) milk and season well. Roughly spread the potato mixture over the fish. Bake in the oven until piping hot and golden-brown.

Plunge the frozen peas into boiling water for 3–4 minutes. Drain well and toss with butter and plenty of black pepper.

Serve the peas at once with the fish pie.

# GREEN LENTIL CASSOULET
## *with 'everything green' salad*

---

Cassoulets are usually based on beans flavoured with different meats. Try this simpler but even more delicious version using green lentils and smoked sausage. Serve it with a refreshing green salad and hunks of crusty bread.

### SERVES 4
*FOR THE GREEN LENTIL CASSOULET*
*8 oz (225 g) green lentils*
*1 tablespoon sunflower oil*
*8 oz (225 g) streaky bacon, rinded and diced*
*1 large onion, peeled and diced*
*2 cloves garlic, peeled and crushed*
*5 fl oz (150 ml) beer or apple juice*
*1 × 14 oz (400 g) tin chopped tomatoes*
*2 tablespoons tomato purée*
*1 teaspoon dried thyme*
*1 bay leaf*
*Salt and freshly ground black pepper*
*8 oz (225 g) smoked sausage, thickly sliced*
*2 oz (50 g) strong Cheddar cheese, grated*
*2 oz (50 g) dried wholemeal breadcrumbs*
*FOR THE 'EVERYTHING GREEN' SALAD*
*1 Iceberg lettuce*
*2 green-skinned eating apples*
*½ cucumber*

Wash the lentils well, place them in a saucepan and cover with cold water. Bring to the boil and simmer gently for about 25 minutes or until just tender but not mushy. Drain the lentils and retain the cooking liquid.

Heat the oil in a pan and fry the diced bacon and onion until golden-brown. Add the garlic, beer (or apple juice), tinned tomatoes, tomato purée, thyme and bay leaf and simmer gently for 10 minutes, stirring occasionally. Season well.

Add the lentils and smoked sausage and 10 fl oz (300 ml) of the reserved lentil cooking liquid. Stir well and cook over a low heat for 25–30 minutes, adding extra liquid if the mixture becomes dry.

Meanwhile, prepare the salad. Wash the ingredients well and dry them. Shred the lettuce into a large salad bowl. Core and chop the eating apples and slice the cucumber. Toss all these well together.

Pile cooked cassoulet into a warm serving dish, scatter over the cheese and breadcrumbs and finish under the grill for 2–3 minutes or until golden and crisp on top. Grind plenty of black pepper over the cassoulet and serve with the salad.

## CHILLI STUFFED TOMATOES

Any left-over cassoulet can be used for stuffing tomatoes. Simply cut large tomatoes in half horizontally and, using a teaspoon, scoop out the centres. Discard the seeds and mix the flesh with the left-over cassoulet. Mix in chilli powder, to taste, with the tomato stuffing. Re-fill the tomatoes with the mixture, sprinkle with a few dried breadcrumbs and bake in the oven pre-heated to gas mark 6, 400°F (200°C), for 10–15 minutes.

# RABBIT WITH PRUNES
### served with potato and parsnip purée

---

Why not give rabbit a try? It's now available ready portioned in some supermarkets – or get your friendly butcher to cut it up for you. This dish can also be made using chicken, but remember to remove the skin.

### SERVES 4
#### FOR THE RABBIT WITH PRUNES
*1 tablespoon sunflower oil*
*1½ lb (750 g) rabbit, cleaned and jointed for 4 people*
*2 oz (50 g) plain flour*
*2 large leeks*
*1 lb (450 g) large carrots, scrubbed and sliced*
*1½ pints (900 ml) chicken stock*
*8 oz (225 g) no-soak prunes*
*Freshly ground black pepper*
*1 clove garlic, peeled and crushed*
*2 teaspoons dried thyme*
*1 bay leaf*

*FOR THE POTATO AND PARSNIP PURÉE*
*2 lb (1 kg) unpeeled floury potatoes, scrubbed and cut into even-sized pieces*
*1 lb (450 g) parsnips, peeled and cut into 2-inch (5-cm) pieces*
*5 fl oz (150 ml) milk*
*Freshly ground black pepper*
*1 teaspoon freshly grated nutmeg*
*2 tablespoons chopped parsley*

Heat the oil in a large saucepan. Toss the rabbit pieces in the flour – enough to coat them all over – and brown them in the hot oil. Add the leeks and carrots and fry all together for a further 2 minutes, turning the rabbit. Add the stock and prunes and season well. Add the garlic, thyme and bay leaf. Bring to the boil, cover and simmer for approximately 50 minutes–1 hour.

Meanwhile, boil the potatoes in a large saucepan until half-cooked. Add the parsnips and continue cooking until both are tender. Drain well, return to the saucepan and mash thoroughly. Add the milk and season with pepper and nutmeg. Spoon into a covered serving dish and keep warm.

To serve the rabbit, remove the lid, season to taste and spoon into a serving dish. Sprinkle the parsley over the potato and parsnip purée and serve with the rabbit to mop up the juices.

# MUSHROOM AND RUNNER BEAN CLAFOUTIS
## *with mustard potatoes and fresh tomato relish*

A savoury version of a pudding traditionally made with a sweet batter.

SERVES 4
*FOR THE CLAFOUTIS*
*8 oz (225 g) runner beans*
*8 oz (225 g) large flat mushrooms, sliced*
*3 eggs*
*3 oz (75 g) plain flour*
*15 fl oz (450 ml) milk*
*4 oz (100 g) blue cheese or Cheddar, grated*
*2 tablespoons brown breadcrumbs*
*Freshly ground black pepper*

*FOR THE TOMATO RELISH*
*1 onion, peeled and sliced*
*1 tablespoon white wine vinegar*
*3 tablespoons sunflower oil*
*1 teaspoon dried thyme*
*1 lb (450 g) tomatoes, cut into thick chunks*
*Freshly ground black pepper*
*FOR THE POTATOES*
*4 large potatoes, washed*
*2 tablespoons wholegrain mustard*
*2 tablespoons sunflower oil*
*1 tablespoon Worcestershire sauce*
*Freshly ground black pepper*
*1 tablespoon chopped parsley*

Pre-heat the oven to gas mark 6, 400°F (200°C).

Cut the potatoes into thick wedges. Place the wedges in a roasting-tin with oil and bake for 30–40 minutes, until crisp on the outside and soft in the centre.

Boil the runner beans for 10 minutes, then drain and place with the mushrooms in a lightly greased, shallow, ovenproof dish.

In a large bowl or liquidiser, combine the eggs, flour and milk together until smooth. Season well. Pour this batter over the runner beans and mushrooms and scatter over the cheese and breadcrumbs. Bake for 40–45 minutes until golden and well risen.

Mix together the mustard, oil and Worcestershire sauce and season with the black pepper. Pour this over the cooked potatoes and toss them in the sauce until they are thoroughly coated. Bake the potatoes for a further 20–25 minutes, turning them occasionally.

Meanwhile, marinade the sliced onions in the vinegar, oil and thyme and allow to stand for 10–15 minutes. Add the roughly chopped tomatoes, season with black pepper and pile into a serving dish.

Remove the clafoutis and the potatoes from the oven. Pile the potatoes into a serving dish and sprinkle with the chopped parsley. Serve the clafoutis straight from its cooking dish, cut into thick wedges. Serve the tomato relish separately.

# SPICED CHICKEN
## *with potatoes in coconut*

---

This spicy chicken dish lends itself well to the sweet chilli coconut potatoes. If you cannot obtain garam masala, ground coriander and turmeric, substitute curry powder to taste. You could serve chapatti or warm
pitta bread too, if you wish.

### SERVES 4
*FOR THE SPICED CHICKEN*
*2 tablespoons sunflower oil*
*2 large onions, peeled and sliced*
*8 chicken thighs or drumsticks, skinned, or 1 × 3–3½ lb (1.5 kg) chicken,*
*jointed into 8 pieces*
*3 teaspoons garam masala*
*2 teaspoons ground coriander*
*2 teaspoons turmeric*
*Freshly ground black pepper*
*2 tablespoons lemon juice*
*15 fl oz (450 ml) water*
*2 tablespoons tomato purée*
*8 oz (225 g) spring greens, finely shredded*
*5 fl oz (150 ml) natural yoghurt*
*FOR THE POTATOES IN COCONUT*
*1 oz (25 g) desiccated coconut*
*10 fl oz (300 ml) semi-skimmed milk*
*2 lb (1 kg) unpeeled potatoes, washed, cut into 1-inch (2.5-cm) pieces and*
*parboiled for 5 minutes*
*3 teaspoons chilli powder*
*1 clove garlic, peeled and crushed*
*1 large bay leaf*
*Freshly ground black pepper*
*1 tablespoon roughly chopped parsley*

Heat the oil in a large saucepan. Add the onions and fry until they are
softened and beginning to brown. Add the skinned pieces of chicken and
toss over a fierce heat for 2–3 minutes. Sprinkle in the spices and seasoning, and cook for a further minute, reducing the heat. Pour in the lemon

juice and water and stir in the tomato purée. Cover and simmer gently for 35–40 minutes, adding extra liquid if the chicken becomes too dry.

Meanwhile, prepare the potato dish. In a saucepan, combine the coconut and milk and heat through. Add the parboiled potatoes, chilli powder, garlic and bay leaf. Simmer gently for 10–15 minutes, until most of the milk has been absorbed but the potatoes are still moist. Season to taste, pile into a serving dish and keep warm.

Remove the lid from the chicken. Toss in the shredded spring greens, replace the lid and cook for 2–3 minutes. Transfer the chicken and greens to a serving dish, spoon over the yoghurt and serve at once. Scatter the chopped parsley over the potatoes and serve with the chicken.

# BARLEY POT
## *with broccoli in tasty tomato sauce*

Pearl barley, which is usually used to thicken soups and stews, here becomes a main ingredient along with vegetables, blue cheese and nuts. If you prefer you can use Cheddar instead of blue cheese.

### SERVES 4
#### *FOR THE BARLEY POT*
*8 oz (225 g) pearl barley*
*8 oz (225 g) sprouted mung beans or bean sprouts*
*1–1½ pints (600–900 ml) vegetable stock*
*1 red pepper, de-seeded and finely sliced*
*1 green pepper, de-seeded and finely sliced*
*1 × 7 oz (200 g) tin sweetcorn, drained*
*1 clove garlic, peeled and crushed (optional)*
*1 bay leaf*
*Freshly ground black pepper*
*4 oz (100 g) blue cheese or Cheddar, crumbled*
*4 oz (100 g) peanuts*
*2 tablespoons chopped parsley*

## FOR THE BROCCOLI IN TASTY TOMATO SAUCE
*1 × 14 oz (400 g) tin chopped tomatoes with herbs*
*1 tablespoon Worcestershire sauce*
*1 lb (450 g) broccoli*
*Freshly ground black pepper*

Wash the barley and soak in cold water for 30 minutes. Drain and place in a saucepan with the mung beans or bean sprouts, vegetable stock, sliced peppers, sweetcorn, garlic (if using) and bay leaf. Season well. Cover with a lid and bring to the boil. Lower the heat and simmer gently for 30–35 minutes or until the barley is just tender, adding extra liquid if necessary during cooking.

Meanwhile, prepare the broccoli dish. In a small saucepan, simmer the tinned chopped tomatoes and Worcestershire sauce for 5 minutes or until reduced by half. Cut the rough ends off the broccoli stalks, divide into florets and cook in boiling water for 4–5 minutes or until just tender. Drain the broccoli, arrange in a warm dish, spoon over the tomato sauce and grind over some black pepper. Keep warm.

When the barley is cooked, gently stir in the cheese and nuts. Pile into a warm serving dish, scatter over the chopped parsley and serve with the broccoli.

# PUDDINGS

PASSION PRUNE PUDDING

AUTUMN PAVLOVA

SPICY MULLED PEARS

WARM PLUM CAKE

PEAR AND GINGER CRUST

CINNAMON TOASTIES WITH WALNUT AND
APPLE MARMALADE

## PASSION PRUNE PUDDING

Deliciously rich, this steamed pudding goes down well with the family.
The grated carrot gives it extra moistness and sweetness.

SERVES 4

*8 oz (225 g) no-soak prunes*
*3 oz (75 g) brown sugar*
*3 oz (75 g) margarine*
*6 oz (175 g) fresh brown breadcrumbs*
*1 teaspoon baking powder*
*1 level teaspoon ground nutmeg*
*1 large egg, separated*
*1 large carrot, grated*
*6 fl oz (175 ml) milk*
*Icing sugar to decorate*

Grease a 1½-pint (900-ml) pudding basin and line the bottom with a disc of
greaseproof paper.

Place the prunes in a pan and barely cover them with water. Cover the
pan and gently simmer for about 10 minutes or until they are plump. Place
the prunes with 3 tablespoons of their juice in the bottom of the basin.

In a mixing bowl beat the sugar and margarine until soft and fluffy. Add the breadcrumbs, baking powder and nutmeg. Now stir in the wet ingredients: the egg yolk, grated carrot and milk.

Whisk the egg white until stiff and fold into the mixture. Spoon the mixture into the basin and cover with a sheet of greaseproof paper and foil. Twist the foil under the basin rim and tie securely with string.

Steam for about 1 hour and 15 minutes and allow the pudding to stand for 15 minutes before serving.

Carefully turn the pudding out, dust lightly with icing sugar and serve warm with fromage frais.

# AUTUMN PAVLOVA

Oaty meringue, topped with fromage frais, apples and apricots: scrumptious! Instead of a large pavlova, you could make small individual meringue nests by placing spoonfuls of the meringue mixture on to the lined baking-tray.

SERVES 4
*3 egg whites*
*6 oz (175 g) brown sugar*
*2 oz (50 g) porridge oats*
*2 teaspoons cornflour*
*1 teaspoon vinegar*
*2 lb (1 kg) Cox's apples*
*8 oz (225 g) dried apricots*
*10 fl oz (300 ml) natural yoghurt*

Pre-heat the oven to gas mark 2, 300°F (150°C). Line a baking-tray with bakewell paper (a must for meringues as greaseproof paper will stick).

In a large, clean bowl, whisk the egg whites until very stiff. Fold in half the sugar and whisk well until very stiff again. Carefully fold in the remaining sugar with the porridge oats, cornflour and vinegar. Pile the mixture on to the prepared baking-tray, level off to a rough 8-inch (20-cm) oval or round, then make a dip in the centre. Bake in the oven for 2 hours.

Core the apples and cut into thick wedges. Chop the apricots. Place both fruit in a saucepan with 3 tablespoons of water and bring to the boil.

Cover and simmer until the fruit is soft, adding extra water if necessary. Remove from the heat and allow to cool.

When the pavlova is cooked, cool on a wire rack and carefully peel off the bakewell paper. To serve, spoon the yoghurt into the centre of the pavlova and top with fruit. Serve straight away.

# SPICY MULLED PEARS

Pears lend themselves well to poaching – gentle cooking gives them much more flavour, especially with the added spices.

### SERVES 4
*10 fl oz (300 ml) orange juice*
*1 bay leaf*
*1 teaspoon ground mixed spice*
*4 cloves*
*1 tablespoon brown sugar*
*6 medium Conference or Comice pears*
*1 × 5 oz (150 g) tin loganberries or raspberries or 6–8 oz (175–225 g)*
*hedgerow berries, lightly cooked*

In a large saucepan, simmer the orange juice, bay leaf, mixed spice, cloves and sugar together for 5 minutes.

Peel the pears and, if necessary, cut a thin slice off the bottoms so that they stand upright. Place them in the saucepan in the syrup. Spoon the berries and their juice over the pears. Cover the saucepan with a large piece of dampened greaseproof paper and a lid. Gently simmer for 35–45 minutes or until the pears are glassy and transparent, basting occasionally.

Place the pears in a serving dish and spoon over the cooking syrup. Serve hot or cold.

# WARM PLUM CAKE

The plums give this cake a good squashy texture. Best eaten warm.

### SERVES 4
*4 oz (100 g) margarine*
*3 oz (75 g) brown sugar*
*2 eggs*
*8 oz (225 g) self-raising wholemeal flour*
*1 lb (450 g) plums, stoned and quartered*
*2 oz (50 g) hazelnuts, chopped*
*Icing sugar to decorate*

Pre-heat the oven to gas mark 5, 375°F (190°C). Grease and line an 8-inch (20-cm) flan dish or cake tin.

Cream together the margarine and sugar really well and then beat in the eggs. Fold in the flour. Carefully fold in the plums and pile the mixture into the prepared dish or tin. Sprinkle the hazelnuts over the top and bake in the oven for 45–50 minutes or until golden-brown on top and firm.

Allow to cool in the dish and, when turning out to serve, dust with icing sugar. Serve slightly warm with fromage frais.

# PEAR AND GINGER CRUST

A truly delicious pear and ginger pudding, best served warm.

### SERVES 4
*2 eggs*
*6 oz (175 g) brown sugar*
*3 tablespoons wholemeal flour*
*1½ teaspoons baking powder*
*2 heaped teaspoons ground ginger*
*3 large ripe pears, cored and diced*
*2 oz (50 g) sultanas*
*2 oz (50 g) flaked almonds*

Pre-heat the oven to gas mark 5, 375°F (190°C). Lightly grease an 8-inch (20-cm) shallow cake tin and dust it out with a little flour.

Whisk the eggs and sugar for 3–4 minutes or until thick and mousse-like. Into this sift the flour, baking powder and ginger and mix until almost blended, taking care not to over mix. Fold in the pears, sultanas and almonds. Pile the mixture into the prepared cake tin and bake for 45–50 minutes or until the top is crisp and brown.

# CINNAMON TOASTIES
## with walnut and apple marmalade

One of my family favourites; it's ideal for a pudding or a teatime treat. You can use any sweet spice for these toasties: ginger, allspice or nutmeg.

### SERVES 4
*1 medium granary or wholemeal French stick*
*5 fl oz (150 ml) milk*
*3 oz (75 g) brown sugar*
*1 egg*
*2 teaspoons ground cinnamon*
*Walnut and Apple Marmalade (see p. 119)*
*Fromage frais to serve*

Pre-heat the grill to a moderate heat. Cut the bread on a slant into $\frac{1}{2}$-inch (1-cm) slices.

In a bowl, whisk together the milk, half the sugar and the egg. Quickly dip the bread slices into the mixture to coat them. Tap the excess mixture off the bread and place the slices on a lightly greased baking-tray. Grill the bread on each side until golden-brown then mix the cinnamon with the rest of the sugar. Dip both sides of the warm toasties in the sugar mixture.

To serve, divide the toasties on to warm plates, spoon on a heap of warm walnut marmalade and top with a little fromage frais. Serve at once.

AUTUMN

# ✦✦ HALLOWE'EN SUPPER ✦✦ SPECIALS

## WITCHES' WINTER CAULDRON

SERVES 6–8 CHILDREN
*1 bay leaf*
*Juice and grated rind of 1 orange*
*1¾ pints (1 litre) very weak tea*
*2 tablespoons runny honey*
*5 fl oz (150 ml) apple juice*
*2 ice cubes*
*6 oz (150 g) black or green grapes, halved and de-seeded*
*2 ripe bananas, peeled and sliced*

Add the bay leaf and the orange juice and rind to the freshly made tea. Pour this into a large jug and chill well. When it is chilled, mix in the honey and apple juice and a couple of ice cubes and set to one side.

To serve, divide the fruit between 6–8 dessert bowls, or tip it into a large punchbowl, and pour over the brew.

## CRACKWHEAT MEATLOAF
*with devilled pimento sauce and roasted root vegetables*

SERVES 4
*FOR THE CRACKWHEAT MEATLOAF*
*2 slices wholemeal bread, soaked in cold water*
*4 oz (100 g) cracked wheat, soaked in cold water for 15 minutes*
*8 oz (225 g) lean minced beef or lamb*
*2 eggs, beaten*
*1 large onion, peeled and grated*
*2 tablespoons soy sauce*
*2 tablespoons tomato purée*
*1 teaspoon dried mixed herbs*
*Freshly ground black pepper*

## FOR THE DEVILLED PIMENTO SAUCE
1 × 14 oz (400 g) tin chopped tomatoes
1 large red pepper, de-seeded and chopped
4 cardamom pods, crushed
2 teaspoons chilli sauce or to taste
## FOR THE ROASTED ROOT VEGETABLES
8 oz (225 g) red potatoes
6 oz (175 g) small turnips
6 oz (175 g) carrots
6 oz (175 g) parsnips
2 tablespoons sunflower oil
1 onion, peeled and chopped
6 cloves garlic, peeled and crushed (optional)
Juice of 1 orange
2 bay leaves
2 tablespoons dried thyme
Freshly ground black pepper

Pre-heat the oven to gas mark 5, 375°F (190°C). Lightly grease a small loaf or cake tin and line the bottom with greaseproof paper.

Squeeze out the bread and drain the cracked wheat. In a large mixing bowl, combine all the meatloaf ingredients together, seasoning well. Pile the mixture into the prepared tin and smooth the top. Cover this with aluminium foil and bake in the oven for 1 hour.

Prepare the root vegetables. Scrub them well (there is no need to peel them unless the skins are badly blemished or tough) and cut them into large even-sized pieces. Heat the oil in a large pan and fry the onion and garlic (if using) for 2–3 minutes. Add the prepared root vegetables and continue to cook for a further 2 minutes. Turn the contents of the pan into a roasting-tin or casserole dish. Pour over the orange juice and sprinkle with the dried herbs. Cover and cook in the oven for 1 hour or until all the vegetables are tender. Season well.

Simmer the sauce ingredients together for 15–20 minutes. Blend in a liquidiser until smooth or push through a sieve. Season to taste.

Remove the meatloaf from the oven and allow it to cool in its tin for about 10 minutes. Turn the loaf out and slice it thickly, arranging the slices on a large, warm platter. Surround this with the roasted vegetables and hand the sauce separately.

## CRISPY MEATLOAF KEBABS

Make these unusual kebabs with left-over meatloaf.

*Crackwheat meatloaf (see previous recipe)*
*Worcestershire sauce*
*Freshly ground black pepper*
*Wholemeal pitta breads*
*Cos lettuce leaves, washed, dried and shredded*
*Cucumber dressing (see p. 121)*

(see p. 121)

Pre-heat the grill.

Cut the cold meatloaf into slices and place on a baking-tray. Sprinkle with Worcestershire sauce and pepper. Place under the grill for 3–4 minutes or until heated through and crisp.

Warm pitta breads under the grill. Split and fill with the lettuce and hot crispy meatloaf. Drizzle over the cucumber dressing and serve straight away.

# GUY FAWKES' SUPPER SPECIAL

## BAKED POTATOES MELODY

Being an outdoor autumn celebration it is not surprising that baked potatoes are a traditional favourite on Guy Fawkes' Night. I have written this recipe with children's firework parties in mind, but you might find that the three fillings given here are equally popular with adults. And you don't *have* to wait for Guy Fawkes' Night to enjoy them!

### SERVES 6–8 CHILDREN
*8 unpeeled medium potatoes, scrubbed*
### FOR THE CREAMY TOMATO FILLING
*3 tomatoes, chopped*
*1 punnet mustard and cress, washed and dried*
*4 tablespoons fromage frais*
*1 tablespoon tomato ketchup*

## *FOR THE HAM AND CUCUMBER FILLING*

½ *cucumber, grated*
2 *teaspoons Marmite*
4 *tablespoons fromage frais*
3 *slices lean ham, shredded*

## *FOR THE SPICY CARROT FILLING*

2 *carrots, scrubbed and grated*
2 *teaspoons curry paste*
8 oz *(225 g) low-fat cream cheese*
1 *tablespoon orange juice*

Pre-heat the oven to gas mark 5, 375°F (190°C). Lightly grease a baking-tray. Prick the potatoes with a fork. Place them on the baking-tray and bake for about 1½ hours or until soft inside.

Prepare the three fillings by simply combining the ingredients for each one in a separate bowl.

Split the potatoes down the centre and pull apart slightly. Fill them with the different filling mixtures and arrange them on a serving dish or in a large basket lined with a clean cloth, for everyone to help themselves.

# WINTER

For winter days, fuel your body with the food that will give you plenty of energy such as root vegetables which are full of flavour and make excellent fillers for soups, goulashes, hot pots and casseroles.

Try the underrated vegetable curly kale because it is inexpensive, tasty and nourishing. Cook it quickly by plunging it into boiling salted water. Kale goes well with garlic, nutmeg and bacon, or try it in a potato-based soup.

Pulses are another energy-giving food and make excellent soups and bakes. There are many different varieties for you to choose from. My favourite are butter beans combined with red cabbage to make a delicious Italian Zuppa (pp. 89–90).

Satsumas, cranberries and a wide selection of nuts and dried fruits make irresistible winter puddings. They are available all year round, but this is the season when they are plentiful and therefore at their cheapest. If you are tired of mince pies you must try the delicious Tarte Tatin made with apples and mincemeat (see p.108).

January brings Burns' Night which is when the Scots celebrate the birth of the poet Robert Burns. The traditional supper is haggis, tatties (potatoes) and 'neeps' (mashed swede). Here I have created a recipe for a vegetarian haggis using lentils, vegetables, oats and barley topped with leek sauce.

# WINTER SPECIALS

If you have to feed family and friends over the Christmas holidays, you will find plenty of recipes to come to the rescue.

For something a bit different on Christmas day, try the Russian turkey pie or, if you like to have a traditional meal, try it for a Boxing Day feast. There's also a lighter version of Christmas pudding that can be made on Christmas Eve or even on the day itself.

## *FESTIVE SPECIALS*

RUSSIAN TURKEY PIE WITH ROAST POTATOES IN THEIR SKINS, GLAZED BRUSSELS SPROUTS AND CARROT CREAM (pp. 111–112)

MUSHROOM HAGGIS, POTATOES COOKED IN THEIR SKINS AND SAUCY LEEKS (pp. 113–114)

HOME-MADE SPICE PUDDING (p. 114)

## *SEASONAL VEGETABLES*

| | | |
|---|---|---|
| Broccoli | Cauliflower | Red cabbage |
| Brussels sprouts | Celery | Swede |
| Brussel tops | Kale | Sweet potatoes |
| Cabbage/greens | Leeks | |
| Carrots | Parsnips | |

## *SEASONAL FRUITS*

| | | |
|---|---|---|
| Brazil nuts | Cranberries | Pears |
| Chestnuts | Dried fruits | Pineapples |
| Clementines | Hazelnuts | Satsumas |
| Cob nuts | Mandarins | Walnuts |
| Cox's apples | Oranges | |

## *SEASONAL FISH*

| | | |
|---|---|---|
| Herrings | Mussels | Whiting |
| Mackerel | Sprats | |

## *SEASONAL MEAT*

Turkey

# LIGHT SUPPERS AND LUNCHES

ITALIAN GARLIC AND BUTTER BEAN ZUPPA

TURKEY AND LEEK BROTH WITH BARLEY

CURLY KALE SOUP WITH HOT MUSTARD AND CHEESE BREAD

PARSNIP GOULASH WITH HERBY DUMPLINGS

SESAME VEGETABLES WITH RAITA

SMOKY FISH SOUFFLÉ

SPANISH-STYLE POTATOES WITH A HOT TOMATO DRESSING

## ITALIAN GARLIC AND BUTTER BEAN ZUPPA

This gutsy Italian dish is more like a stew than a soup and makes a welcoming meal for a cold winter's day. Serve with hunks of warm granary bread.

### SERVES 4

*8 oz (225 g) butter beans, soaked overnight in cold water*
*1 tablespoon sunflower oil*
*3 cloves garlic, peeled and crushed*
*12 oz (350 g) white or red cabbage, washed and shredded*
*1 bay leaf*
*2 pints (1.2 litres) vegetable stock*
*2 oz (50 g) mature Cheddar or Parmesan cheese, grated*
*Juice and grated rind of 1 lemon*
*2 eggs, hard-boiled and chopped*
*2 tablespoons chopped parsley*
*Freshly ground black pepper*

Drain the butter beans, place in a large saucepan of boiling water and boil for 10 minutes. Drain again.

Heat the oil in a large saucepan and add the crushed garlic and cabbage. Fry for 4 minutes, stirring frequently. Add the butter beans, bay leaf and vegetable stock. Cover and simmer gently for 1½ hours, adding extra stock (or water) if necessary.

Mix together the cheese, lemon rind, chopped eggs and parsley and set to one side. Season the soup with lemon juice and black pepper and ladle into large soup bowls. Scatter over the cheese and parsley mixture and serve.

This soup develops an even better flavour when warmed up 1 or 2 days later, which means that you can prepare it in advance. Alternatively, you can thin the soup down with stock or water to make an ideal tasty sauce to accompany pasta.

# TURKEY AND LEEK BROTH WITH BARLEY

Make sure you use the green tops of the leeks as well as the white parts, because they add lots of extra flavour. Pearl barley is the traditional thickener for broths, though brown rice makes a good alternative.

### SERVES 4–6
1 tablespoon sunflower oil
1½ lb (750 g) leeks, washed and shredded
1 lb (450 g) turnips, peeled and finely sliced
2 teaspoons ground ginger
2 pints (1.2 litres) chicken stock
5 fl oz (150 ml) orange juice
4 oz (100 g) pearl barley
1 bay leaf
Freshly ground black pepper
8 oz (225 g) cooked turkey, shredded
Chopped parsley to garnish

In a large pan, heat the oil and gently fry the leeks and turnips until softened. Sprinkle on the ginger and cook for 30 seconds. Pour in the stock and orange juice. Scatter in the pearl barley and add the bay leaf. Season well. Bring the soup to the boil and simmer for 35–40 minutes or until the barley is tender. Add the cooked turkey, re-heat thoroughly and check the seasoning, adjusting as necessary. Ladle the broth into soup bowls and garnish with plenty of chopped parsley.

# CURLY KALE SOUP
*with hot mustard and cheese bread*

Kale, one of the earliest forms of cabbage, is full of vitamins. It is known by many names – Scotch kale, curly kale and bone kale to mention but a few. Just wash and shred the curly leaves and add to this simple soup at the last moment to give a delicious texture.

### SERVES 4
*1 tablespoon sunflower oil*
*1 clove garlic, peeled and crushed*
*2 tablespoons turmeric*
*1½ lb (750 g) unpeeled potatoes, washed and cut into even-sized pieces*
*1½ pints (900 ml) vegetable stock*
*Freshly ground black pepper*
*5 fl oz (150 ml) whole milk*
*8 oz (225 g) curly kale*
*FOR THE HOT MUSTARD AND CHEESE BREAD*
*1 small onion, peeled and finely chopped*
*1 tablespoon chopped parsley*
*3 tablespoons sunflower oil*
*4 oz (100 g) Red Leicester cheese, grated*
*1 tablespoon French mustard*
*Freshly ground black pepper*
*1 granary French stick*

In a large saucepan, heat the oil and gently fry the garlic and turmeric for 1 minute. Add the potatoes and stock and season well. Bring to the boil, cover and simmer for 25–30 minutes or until the potatoes are tender.

While the soup is cooking, prepare the bread. Pre-heat the oven to gas mark 6, 400°F (200°C).

In a bowl, mix together the onion, parsley, oil, cheese, mustard and pepper. Cut the French stick into 1-inch (2.5-cm)-thick slices without cutting right through, so that they are still joined together at the base. Spread the cut slices with the mustard and cheese mixture. Wrap in aluminium foil and bake in the oven for 10–15 minutes. Alternatively you can toast separate slices under the grill, spread on the mixture and toast again – as for Welsh rarebit.

Purée the soup in a blender and return it to the pan. Pour in the milk and season again to taste. Finely shred the kale and add it to the soup. Simmer for a further 4–5 minutes and serve accompanied by the hot bread.

# PARSNIP GOULASH
## *with herby dumplings*

These herby dumplings turn a simple goulash into a warming winter starter or a light lunch or supper dish.

### SERVES 6 AS A STARTER OR 4 AS A LIGHT MAIN COURSE
1 tablespoon sunflower oil
1 large clove garlic, peeled and crushed
1 large onion, peeled and chopped
2 lb (1 kg) parsnips, peeled and coarsely chopped
2 tablespoons paprika
2 teaspoons plain flour
1 × 14 oz (400 g) tin chopped tomatoes
1 tablespoon tomato purée
1½ pints (900 ml) vegetable stock
2 teaspoons dried thyme
1 bay leaf
Freshly ground black pepper
FOR THE HERBY DUMPLINGS
2 oz (50 g) margarine
4 oz (100 g) self-raising flour
2 oz (50 g) porridge oats
2 oz (50 g) strong Cheddar cheese
1 tablespoon chopped parsley
Freshly ground black pepper
About 5 fl oz (150 ml) cold water

In a large saucepan or frying-pan, heat the oil and gently fry the garlic and onion until golden. Add the parsnips and paprika, sprinkle over the flour and cook gently for a minute or two before adding the remaining ingredients. Cover and simmer very gently for about 50 minutes.

In a bowl, rub the margarine into the flour and oats. Add the cheese and parsley and season with black pepper. Add enough cold water to make a smooth dough and divide into 12 dumplings. About 10 minutes before the end of the goulash's cooking time, pop the dumplings on to the goulash, so that they float on top. Replace the lid and simmer for a further 8–10 minutes.

# SESAME VEGETABLES WITH RAITA

Hot and spicy vegetables with cooling raita to come to your rescue. Serve with popadums, pitta bread or nan.

### SERVES 4–6 AS A STARTER OR
### 4 AS A LIGHT LUNCH OR SUPPER DISH
*1 large onion, peeled and sliced*
*1 large swede, peeled and cut into chip-like sticks*
*1 tablespoon sunflower oil*
*2 tablespoons tandoori or tikka paste*
*About 10 fl oz (300 ml) vegetable stock*
*8 oz (225 g) frozen runner beans*
*1 clove garlic, peeled and crushed*
*1 lb (450 g) spring greens, washed and finely shredded*
*2 tablespoons sesame seeds*
*FOR THE RAITA*
*1 large onion, peeled and grated*
*2 teaspoons mint sauce*
*10 fl oz (300 ml) natural yoghurt*
*Freshly ground black pepper*

In a large frying-pan or wok, fry the onion and swede in the oil for 2–3 minutes. Add the tandoori or tikka paste and vegetable stock. Cover and simmer for 7–10 minutes or until the swede is tender but still slightly firm to the bite.

Mix the raita ingredients together and set to one side.

To the vegetables add the frozen runner beans, cover and cook for a further 5 minutes, adding extra liquid if necessary. Toss in the garlic and spring greens at the last moment and heat through for 2–3 minutes. Scatter with the sesame seeds and serve straight from the pan with the raita and bread suggested in the introduction to this recipe.

## *SPICY PASTIES*

Make these warming pasties with cooked vegetables left over from the above recipe. Simply wrap them in pastry, brush with beaten egg or milk and bake in the oven at gas mark 6, 400°F (200°C), until golden-brown. Serve warm.

# SMOKY FISH SOUFFLÉ

Don't let the word soufflé send you running and screaming from the kitchen. Try this easy and quick soufflé omelette, served with chunks of warm crusty bread and salad.

### SERVES 4
*1½ oz (40 g) butter*
*1 teaspoon freshly grated nutmeg*
*1½ oz (40 g) plain flour*
*10 fl oz (300 ml) semi-skimmed milk*
*8 oz (225 g) carrots, scrubbed and grated*
*8 oz (225 g) peppered mackerel fillets, skinned and flaked*
*Freshly ground black pepper*
*5 eggs, separated*
*2 tablespoons sunflower oil*
*1 heaped tablespoon dried wholemeal breadcrumbs*

Heat the butter in a small saucepan with the nutmeg. Add the flour and cook gently for 1 minute. Remove the pan from the heat and pour in the milk. Mix well until smooth, then return the pan to the heat. Bring to the boil, stirring constantly, and simmer over a low heat for 2–3 minutes to cook the flour. Add the grated carrots and flaked mackerel. Taste and season if necessary. Set to one side to cool slightly.

Pre-heat the grill.

Add the egg yolks to the fish mixture and blend well. In a large dry bowl, whisk the egg whites until stiff and fold into the fish mixture. Heat the sunflower oil in a large frying-pan and pour in the soufflé mixture. Cook over a medium heat until the base of the soufflé is golden. Scatter over the breadcrumbs and finish the soufflé under the grill for about 8–10 minutes (reducing the heat if necessary) until risen, golden and firm to the touch. Take care that the handle of the pan does not burn. Serve at once, straight from the pan.

This soufflé mixture can also be cooked in individual ramekins or teacups. Set them in a roasting-tin half-filled with boiling water and bake in the oven at gas mark 4, 350°F (180°C), for 20–25 minutes or until puffed and just firm. Turn out and serve immediately.

Cold soufflé omelette is delicious eaten cold like a quiche, with a light salad. Alternatively, you can re-heat it under the grill, topped with sliced tomatoes, and serve it on toast.

## SPANISH-STYLE POTATOES
### with a hot tomato dressing

Get out of the habit of peeling potatoes. They hold together better and taste even more delicious with their skins on. Serve with crisp salad leaves.

### SERVES 4
*2 lb (1 kg) unpeeled potatoes, washed*
*2 tablespoons sunflower oil*
*1 large onion, peeled and sliced*
*1 clove garlic, peeled and crushed*
*2 tablespoons Worcestershire sauce*
*Juice and grated rind of 1 lemon*
*1 large red pepper, de-seeded and sliced*
*1 × 14 oz (400 g) tin chopped tomatoes with herbs*
*2 bay leaves*
*3 teaspoons tabasco sauce*
*Freshly ground black pepper*
*Chopped parsley to garnish*

Pre-heat the oven to gas mark 6, 400°F (200°C).

Cut the potatoes into wedges or thick slices. Place in a roasting-tin and mix with the oil, onion, garlic and Worcestershire sauce. Bake in the oven for about 50 minutes–1 hour or until the potatoes are crisp on the outside and tender inside.

In a small mixing bowl, combine the red pepper, tomatoes, bay leaves, Tabasco sauce, and juice and rind of the lemon. Spoon it over the crisply cooked potatoes. Grind over plenty of black pepper and return to the oven for a further 20–25 minutes. Serve hot, sprinkled with chopped parsley.

Cold left-over potatoes make a great base for a Spanish tortilla. Just add a couple of eggs and some dried mixed herbs and cook as for an omelette for another Spanish feast.

# MAIN COURSES

MACKEREL RAGOÛT WITH NUTMEG NOODLES AND BROCCOLI

LEEK AND MUSTARD GNOCCHI WITH PEASANT TOMATO SAUCE AND STIR-FRY GREENS

PORK AND APPLE COBBLER WITH PARSNIPS AND STEAMED KALE

GOLDEN COURGETTE RISOTTO WITH COUNTRY-STYLE TOMATOES AND STIR-FRY GREENS

POTATO AND CELERY RÖSTI WITH TOMATO AND THYME SAUCE AND STEAMED BROCCOLI AND CAULIFLOWER

BEETROOT AND BEEF DAUBE, BAKED POTATOES TOPPED WITH WHITE CHEESE AND GLAZED BRUSSELS SPROUTS

# MACKEREL RAGOÛT
## *with nutmeg noodles and broccoli*

---

Baking is one of the best ways of cooking mackerel. Try this winter fish casserole to warm the cockles of your heart.

### SERVES 4
### *FOR THE MACKEREL RAGOÛT*
*2 tablespoons sunflower oil*
*1 large onion, peeled and sliced*
*1 lb (450 g) large carrots, scrubbed and grated*
*½ head celery, washed and chopped*
*1 clove garlic, peeled and crushed*
*2 teaspoons dill seed or 2 tablespoons chopped fresh dill weed*
*Freshly ground black pepper*
*2 medium mackerel, filleted*
*1 × 14 oz (400 g) tin chopped tomatoes with herbs*
*Juice and grated rind of 1 orange*
*1 bay leaf*
*1 tablespoon dried wholemeal breadcrumbs*
*Chopped parsley to garnish*
### *FOR THE NUTMEG NOODLES*
*12 oz (350 g) dried noodles*
*1 tablespoon sunflower oil*
*Freshly grated nutmeg*
*Freshly ground black pepper*
### *FOR THE BROCCOLI*
*12 oz (350 g) broccoli*

Pre-heat the oven to gas mark 5, 375°F (190°C).

In a large frying-pan, heat the oil and gently fry the vegetables (onions, carrots and celery) until softened. Remove from the heat and add the garlic and dill seed. Season with pepper and spoon into an ovenproof dish. Lay over the mackerel fillets, skin side up (this will prevent the fish from drying out). Pour over the tomatoes and orange juice and add the orange rind and bay leaf. Sprinkle evenly with the breadcrumbs and grind over some black pepper. Bake in the oven, uncovered, for 20–25 minutes.

Twelve minutes before serving, plunge the noodles into boiling water and cook gently for 6–7 minutes or until tender but still slightly firm to the bite.

Prepare the broccoli by steaming or boiling.

Drain the noodles, return them to the saucepan with the oil and toss over a high heat. Season with nutmeg and black pepper.

Remove the baked mackerel from the oven. Scatter with parsley and serve with the accompanying dishes.

# LEEK AND MUSTARD GNOCCHI
## with peasant tomato sauce and stir-fry greens

*Gnocchi* is Italian for dumpling. It can be made using potatoes, semolina or eggs. Try these baked gnocchi which are delicious flavoured with leeks and cheese.

### SERVES 4
#### FOR THE LEEK AND MUSTARD GNOCCHI
*1 lb (450 g) leeks, washed and shredded*
*2 pints (1.2 litres) semi-skimmed milk*
*7 oz (200 g) semolina*
*5 oz (150 g) mature Cheddar or Cheshire cheese, grated*
*1 tablespoon wholegrain mustard*
*Freshly ground black pepper*
*1 large egg, beaten*
*A little sunflower oil*
#### FOR THE PEASANT TOMATO SAUCE
*1 × 1 lb (450 g) carton creamed tomatoes*
*2 large fresh tomatoes, chopped*
*1 teaspoon brown sugar*
*2 teaspoons Worcestershire sauce*
*1 teaspoon dried thyme*
*Freshly ground black pepper*
#### FOR THE STIR-FRY GREENS
*1 tablespoon sunflower oil*
*1½ lb (750 g) greens, washed and shredded*
*Freshly ground black pepper*

Pre-heat the oven to gas mark 6, 400°F (200°C).

Poach half of the leeks in the milk, until soft. Lower the heat and add the semolina, pouring it slowly in a controlled stream. Beat well until very thick for about 6–8 minutes. Fold in half of the grated cheese followed by the mustard, and season with pepper. Mix in the beaten egg and blend well.

Moisten a large plate or baking-tray with water and spoon out the gnocchi mixture. Using wet hands or a flat knife, shape and spread the mixture out to the thickness of 1 inch (2.5 cm). Allow to cool.

Using a biscuit cutter, egg cup or small glass, cut the gnocchi mixture into rounds. Lightly grease an ovenproof dish with oil and place the disc trimmings in the bottom. Scatter with half the remaining shredded leeks and drizzle over a little sunflower oil. Lay the cut-out rounds on top and scatter with the remaining leeks and cheese. Season and bake in the oven for 20–25 minutes or until a crust has formed; if you wish, you can finish the dish under the grill at the last moment.

In a saucepan, combine the sauce ingredients together and simmer for 10–12 minutes. Season to taste.

Heat the oil in a frying-pan or wok and stir-fry the greens until steaming but crisp. Season. Serve at once with the gnocchi and peasant tomato sauce.

## *TOASTED GNOCCHI*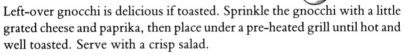

Left-over gnocchi is delicious if toasted. Sprinkle the gnocchi with a little grated cheese and paprika, then place under a pre-heated grill until hot and well toasted. Serve with a crisp salad.

# PORK AND APPLE COBBLER
## with parsnips and steamed kale

Apples, lentils and pork topped with a herby crust make this a classic English cobbler. Smoked bacon or ham is a good substitute for the pork.

SERVES 4
FOR THE PORK AND APPLE COBBLER
8 oz (225 g) split red lentils, washed
1 large onion, peeled and chopped
1 bay leaf
1½ pints (900 ml) vegetable stock
8 oz (225 g) lean pork, diced
1 lb (450 g) eating apples, cored and thickly sliced
2 teaspoons ground cumin (optional)
Freshly ground black pepper
4 oz (100 g) granary or wholemeal flour
4 oz (100 g) self-raising flour
2 oz (50 g) margarine
2 teaspoons dried mixed herbs
About 5 fl oz (150 ml) semi-skimmed milk
FOR THE PARSNIPS AND STEAMED KALE
2 lb (1 kg) parsnips, peeled and quartered
1 tablespoon sunflower oil
1½ lb (750 g) curly kale, washed
Freshly ground black pepper

Pre-heat the oven to gas mark 5, 375°F (190°C).

Place the lentils, onion and bay leaf in a large saucepan and cover with vegetable stock. Bring to the boil and simmer for 20–25 minutes or until the lentils are soft.

Meanwhile, dry-fry the diced pork in a frying-pan for 1–2 minutes. Toss in the apple slices and cook over a fierce heat for a further 2 minutes. Stir in the cumin (if using) and season with pepper. Remove from the heat and mix with the cooked lentils. Spoon the mixture into a shallow oven-proof dish.

For the scone topping, sift together the flours and rub in the margarine with your fingertips. Stir in the herbs and add enough milk to make a soft dough. Roll out on a floured surface to ½ inch (1-cm) thickness. Place the dough on top of the pork and apple mixture. Mark the dough with a lattice (criss-cross) pattern. Brush with milk and bake in the oven for 25–30 minutes or until the topping is golden-brown.

Place the prepared parsnips in water and boil for about 12–15 minutes or until tender. Heat the oil in a large saucepan, add the kale and cover with dampened greaseproof paper and a lid. Lower the heat and steam gently for 8–10 minutes.

Arrange the kale on a large serving dish with the parsnips. Season. Remove the cobbler from the oven and serve at once with the vegetables.

# GOLDEN COURGETTE RISOTTO
## *with country-style tomatoes and stir-fry greens*

Risotto is an Italian way of cooking rice. It is not a way of re-heating cooked rice with fresh ingredients, which can be tasty but not a patch on the real thing. Risotto can be made with many different flavourings and ingredients added to the rice while it cooks. Here is just one of those variations. Serve it with warm crusty bread to mop up the delicious juices.

### SERVES 4
*FOR THE GOLDEN COURGETTE RISOTTO*
*1 tablespoon sunflower oil*
*4 rashers lean bacon, rinded and diced*
*1 large onion, peeled and finely chopped*
*3 large courgettes, finely chopped*
*1 garlic clove, peeled and crushed*
*1 tablespoon turmeric*
*14 oz (400 g) Italian easy-cook brown rice or risotto rice*
*Freshly ground black pepper*
*1 bay leaf*
*2 pints (1.2 litres) vegetable or chicken stock*
*4 oz (100 g) Red Leicester cheese, grated*
*Chopped parsley to garnish*

*FOR THE COUNTRY-STYLE TOMATOES*
*4 large tomatoes*
*2 tablespoons dried wholemeal breadcrumbs*
*1 teaspoon dried thyme*
*1 tablespoon chopped parsley*
*1 tablespoon sunflower oil*
*Freshly ground black pepper*
*FOR THE STIR-FRY GREENS*
*1 tablespoon sunflower oil*
*2 lb (1 kg) greens, washed and shredded*
*Freshly ground black pepper*

For the risotto, heat the oil in a large frying-pan or wok and add the bacon, onion and courgettes. Fry gently for 3–4 minutes. Add the garlic, sprinkle in the turmeric and rice and fry lightly for a few minutes. Season and add the bay leaf. Add a ladleful of hot stock and stir well, continuing to cook. When almost all the stock has been absorbed, add another ladleful. Keep stirring. Repeat this process until all the stock has been used. The rice will take 30–35 minutes to cook: when the risotto is ready, it should be soft, creamy and fairly thick.

Pre-heat the grill. Cut the tomatoes in half and place cut side *down* in an ovenproof dish. Grill for 2–3 minutes, then turn over using a fish slice. In a small bowl, mix together the breadcrumbs and herbs. Scatter these over the tomatoes and sprinkle with the oil. Season well and place under the hot grill for 3–4 minutes or until the topping is golden and the tomatoes are cooked.

Stir-fry the greens (see p. 98–99).

Stir the cheese into the risotto and serve from the pan, scattered with plenty of chopped parsley and black pepper. Serve the vegetables separately.

## CHILLED RICE MOULDS

Left-over risotto is tasty eaten cold. Simply spoon into lightly greased ramekins or teacups, press down firmly and chill in the refrigerator for 2 hours. Turn out the rice moulds on to plates, garnish with salad and serve with a tasty yoghurt raita (see p. 93–94).

# POTATO AND CELERY RÖSTI
*with tomato and thyme sauce and steamed broccoli and cauliflower*

The potato is our best-known vegetable, but sadly it always seems to play a supporting role. Here is a dish to give it a lead part.

### SERVES 4
*FOR THE POTATO AND CELERY RÖSTI*
*2 lb (1 kg) unpeeled medium waxy potatoes, scrubbed and halved*
*2 tablespoons sunflower oil*
*½ head celery, finely sliced*
*1 large onion, peeled and finely chopped*
*Freshly ground black pepper*
*FOR THE TOMATO AND THYME SAUCE*
*1 × 14 oz (400 g) carton creamed tomatoes*
*2 teaspoons dried thyme*
*2 teaspoons fennel seeds (optional)*
*1 teaspoon brown sugar*
*5 fl oz (150 ml) orange juice*
*Freshly ground black pepper*
*FOR THE STEAMED BROCCOLI AND CAULIFLOWER*
*1 lb (450 g) broccoli*
*1 small cauliflower*
*Freshly ground black pepper*

Parboil the potatoes in water for 7 minutes. Drain and leave to cool. In a frying-pan with a little of the oil, gently fry the celery and onion until soft. Turn them into a mixing bowl and grate in the cooked potatoes. Season well and mix together thoroughly.

Heat 1 tablespoon of the oil in the frying-pan and add the mixture, spreading it out and pressing it down firmly. Cook over a medium heat for about 10–15 minutes or until the underside is crisp and brown. Loosen the underside of the rösti, place a large plate upside down over the pan, invert the pan and tip out the rösti on to the plate. Add a little extra oil to the pan and, when it is hot, slide the rösti back into the pan and cook the other side for a further 10–15 minutes. If you would rather not turn the rösti out of the pan, you can simply finish the uncooked side under the grill.

While the rösti is cooking, simmer the sauce ingredients together for 10–12 minutes and season to taste.

Break the broccoli and cauliflower into even-sized florets and steam until just tender. Season.

Serve the rösti, cut into wedges, from the pan. Hand the sauce and vegetables separately.

Any left-overs can be re-heated in the oven or under the grill and served as a vegetable accompaniment to another main dish.

# BEETROOT AND BEEF DAUBE,
## *baked potatoes topped with white cheese and glazed Brussels sprouts*

Beetroot and beef marry well together – leave the beetroot off the salad plate and try it this way!

### SERVES 4
### *FOR THE BEETROOT AND BEEF DAUBE*
*1 large onion, peeled and chopped*
*1 tablespoon sunflower oil*
*8 oz (225 g) stewing beef, cubed*
*1 clove garlic, peeled and crushed*
*12 oz (350 g) beetroot, cooked, peeled and diced*
*1 bay leaf*
*Freshly ground black pepper*
*1½ oz (40 g) plain flour*
*5 fl oz (150 ml) beer*
*1 pint (600 ml) vegetable stock*
*Chopped parsley to garnish*
### *FOR THE BAKED POTATOES TOPPED WITH WHITE CHEESE*
*4 baking potatoes, washed*
*1 × 5 oz (150 g) carton fromage frais*
*Freshly ground black pepper*

## *FOR THE GLAZED BRUSSELS SPROUTS*

*1½ lb (750 g) Brussels sprouts, prepared*
*1 tablespoon sunflower oil*
*2 tablespoons honey*
*Freshly ground black pepper*

Pre-heat the oven to gas mark 4, 350°F (180°C).

In a saucepan, gently fry the onion in the oil until golden and softened. Add the beef and toss over a fierce heat to seal the meat. Stir in the garlic, beetroot and bay leaf and season well. Reduce the heat. Sprinkle over the flour and pour on the beer and stock, mixing very well and bringing to the boil. Transfer the contents of the saucepan to a casserole dish, place the casserole in the oven and cook for 2 hours.

Prick the potatoes with a fork and put them in a roasting-tin. Bake in the oven for 1–1½ hours or until tender.

Prepare the glazed Brussels sprouts (see pp. 111–112).

When you are ready to serve, split the baked potatoes, fill with the fromage frais and season well with pepper. Mix any left-over fromage frais with a little water or milk and drizzle over the daube. Sprinkle the daube with chopped parsley and serve with the potatoes and glazed sprouts.

# PUDDINGS

CLEMENTINE AND CHESTNUT CRUMBLE

WHOLE APPLE PIE

APPLE AND MINCEMEAT TARTE TATIN

GRILLED ORANGES WITH ALMOND BISCUITS

RHUBARB AND GINGER PIE

## CLEMENTINE AND CHESTNUT CRUMBLE

Tangy clementines and rich chestnuts are a favourite of mine at Christmas time. Here they are combined together to make a crumble with a difference. Serve warm with custard sauce (see p. 124) or fromage frais.

SERVES 4

*1 lb (450 g) clementines or satsumas*
*8 oz (225 g) chestnuts, pierced with a knife*
*8 oz (225 g) dried dates, split and stoned*
*8 fl oz (250 ml) orange juice*
*5 fl oz (150 ml) water*
*FOR THE TOPPING*
*3 oz (75 g) porridge oats*
*3 oz (75 g) granary or wholemeal flour*
*3 oz (75 g) demerara sugar*
*3 tablespoons sunflower oil*

Pre-heat the oven to gas mark 6, 400°F (200°C).

Peel the clementines or satsumas and pull them into segments. Place them in an ovenproof dish. Plunge the pierced chestnuts into boiling water and cook for 5 minutes. Allow to cool a little, then peel while still warm (otherwise the skins will be hard to remove). Toss the chestnuts and split dates with the clementines and pour the orange juice and water over them.

In a large mixing bowl, combine all the dry ingredients for the topping. Pour on the sunflower oil, a little at a time, and rub together gently with your fingertips. Scatter the mixture over the fruit and bake in the oven for 35–40 minutes or until bubbling hot and golden-brown.

# WHOLE APPLE PIE

Traditionally apple pie was served with hunks of cheese. To incorporate cheese into this recipe, you could replace the prunes with a little grated cheese.

SERVES 4–6
*4 medium Bramley cooking apples, peeled and cored*
*8 oz (225 g) prunes, chopped*
*2 tablespoons runny honey*
*10 fl oz (300 ml) water*
*½ oz (15 g) caster sugar*
*1 teaspoon ground cinnamon*
*8 oz (225 g) ready-made shortcrust pastry*

Pre-heat the oven to gas mark 6, 400°F (200°C).

Place the whole peeled apples in a deep pie-dish. Stuff the apples with the chopped prunes. Pour over the runny honey and water and set to one side.

Mix the sugar and cinnamon together. Roll out the pastry on a floured surface and cover the apples with the pastry. Sprinkle over the cinnamon mixture and trim the edges, using the trimmings to decorate the top of the pie. Bake in the oven for 10–15 minutes or until the pastry is golden. Reduce the oven temperature to gas mark 4, 350°F (180°C), for a further 40–45 minutes to allow the apples to cook through. Serve warm.

Alternatively you could make individual whole apple pies or apple dumplings by simply wrapping the stuffed apples individually in pastry and baking at gas mark 5, 375°F (190°C), for 30–35 minutes. You will probably need 1 lb (450 g) of pastry and you will not need to use the water as in the main recipe.

# APPLE AND MINCEMEAT TARTE TATIN

Fed up with mince pies at Christmas? Try this yummy tart, which is served upside down: delicious with fromage frais or Greek yoghurt.

SERVES 4
*2 lb (1 kg) eating apples*
*8 oz (225 g) mincemeat*
*5 oz (150 g) rice flour or semolina*
*5 oz (150 g) granary or plain flour*
*4 oz (100 g) margarine*
*1 large egg, beaten*

Pre-heat the oven to gas mark 6, 400°F (200°C). Lightly grease a 10-inch (25-cm) shallow cake tin or flan dish.

The apples can be peeled or left unpeeled; core them and cut into thick slices. Combine the apples with the mincemeat and turn into the prepared tin or dish. Set to one side.

In a large mixing bowl, combine the flours and rub in the margarine until the mixture resembles coarse breadcrumbs. Add the beaten egg to bind the ingredients together to form a soft but not sticky dough – you may need to add a little cold water too. Roll the pastry out on a floured surface into an 11-inch (28-cm) round. Place the pastry over the apple mixture and, with a sharp knife, tidy the edges. Bake in the oven for 35–40 minutes or until the pastry is very crisp and the apples are just tender.

Remove the pudding from the oven and allow to stand for 10 minutes. Carefully invert a large plate over the cake tin and turn out the pudding. Serve warm.

# GRILLED ORANGES
## *with almond biscuits*

---

This recipe is quick and easy. The almond biscuits are very simple to make, though you could, of course, substitute ready-made muesli-style biscuits. Grapefruit and bananas make a good alternative to the oranges.

### SERVES 4
*5 large oranges*
*1 tablespoon demerara sugar*
*2 teaspoons freshly grated nutmeg (optional)*
*FOR THE ALMOND BISCUITS*
*3 oz (75 g) margarine*
*2 oz (50 g) plain flour*
*2 oz (50 g) porridge oats*
*3 oz (75 g) light soft brown sugar*
*2 oz (50 g) flaked almonds*
*1 level teaspoon bicarbonate of soda, dissolved in 1 tablespoon boiling water*

Pre-heat the oven to gas mark 5, 375°F (190°C). Lightly grease a shallow ovenproof dish and a baking-tray.

Carefully cut the peel and pith away from the oranges with a sharp knife. Slice them thinly across into rounds and arrange them, slightly overlapping, in the prepared dish. Place the dish in the freezer for 30 minutes.

To make the biscuits, mix all the ingredients together in a bowl to form a dough. Place teaspoons of the dough on the baking-tray, keeping them well apart, and press each one out using the back of a teaspoon – you should have enough dough for 10 biscuits. Bake in the oven for 15–20 minutes or until golden-brown. Cool the biscuits on the baking-tray until they harden, then finish cooling on a wire rack.

Mix the demerara sugar and nutmeg together. Remove the oranges from the freezer. Scatter with the spiced sugar and grill for 3–4 minutes until the sugar has melted.

To serve, arrange the orange slices on a dessert plate with the fromage frais and place a warm almond biscuit on the side. Serve immediately.

# RHUBARB AND GINGER PIE

Rhubarb pie, my favourite pudding from childhood days – you can't beat it! Serve with custard sauce (see p. 124) or fromage frais.

### SERVES 4
*1½ lb (750 g) rhubarb, cut into 1-inch (2.5-cm) lengths*
*1 teaspoon ground ginger*
*3–4 tablespoons honey*
*1 tablespoon cold water*
*8 oz (225 g) ready-made wholemeal shortcrust pastry*
*Milk to glaze*
*Caster sugar to dust*

Pre-heat the oven to gas mark 6, 400°F (200°C).

Mix together the rhubarb, ginger, honey and water and turn into a 2-pint (1.2-litre) pie dish. Place a pie-funnel or an upturned eggcup in the centre of the dish and set to one side.

On a floured surface, roll out the pastry to fit the top of the pie-dish and trim. Cut the trimmings into strips. Brush the rim of the pie-dish with water, lay the strips of pastry around the rim and brush again with water. Using a floured rolling pin, pick up the pastry lid and lay it over the rhubarb, pressing the edges firmly down on to the pastry-covered rim of the dish. Trim the edges again if necessary and crimp if desired. Make a slit in the centre of the pie (to allow steam to escape) and decorate with any remaining pastry trimmings cut into leaves. Brush with milk and dust with caster sugar. Bake in the oven for about 15 minutes, then turn the oven down to gas mark 4, 350°F (180°C), and cook for a further 20–30 minutes. The pastry should be very crisp and golden and the rhubarb cooked through. Serve hot or warm.

# FESTIVE SPECIALS

## RUSSIAN TURKEY PIE
*with roast potatoes in their skins, glazed Brussels sprouts and carrot cream*

---

This festive meal makes a great alternative to roast turkey at Christmas time. If you wish to make it completely vegetarian, use 1 lb (450 g) chestnuts in place of the turkey.

### SERVES 4
*FOR THE RUSSIAN TURKEY PIE*
*1 tablespoon sunflower oil*
*1 large onion, peeled and chopped*
*2 teaspoons dried sage*
*8 oz (225 g) fresh or frozen (defrosted) cranberries*
*8 oz (225 g) turkey leg meat, cooked and flaked*
*3 eggs, hard-boiled and chopped*
*8 oz (225 g) cooked brown rice*
*4 tablespoons natural yoghurt*
*Freshly ground black pepper*
*1 lb (450 g) ready-made puff pastry*
*1 egg, beaten*
*FOR THE ROAST POTATOES IN THEIR SKINS*
*1½ lb (750 g) unpeeled medium potatoes*
*2 tablespoons sunflower oil*
*1 clove garlic, peeled and crushed*
*Salt and freshly ground black pepper*
*FOR THE GLAZED BRUSSELS SPROUTS*
*1½ lb (750 g) Brussels sprouts*
*1 tablespoon sunflower oil*
*2 tablespoons honey*
*Freshly ground black pepper*
*FOR THE CARROT CREAM*
*2 lb (1 kg) large carrots, peeled and sliced*
*Freshly ground black pepper*

For the pie, heat the oil in a saucepan, add the onion and sage and fry gently for 2–3 minutes. Add the cranberries, cover and cook for 4 minutes or until the berries burst. Set to one side to cool.

In a large bowl combine the turkey, hard-boiled eggs, rice and yoghurt, then stir in the onion mixture. Season well.

Roll out the pastry on a floured surface and form it into a rectangle 12 × 20 inches (30 × 50 cm), trimming the edges to make them even. Place on a floured baking-tray.

Spoon the filling down the centre of the pastry, leaving a gap of 2 inches (5-cm) at each end. Fold over the ends and wrap and enclose the pastry around the filling. Use the pastry trimmings for decoration and make 2 small slits in the top of the pie to allow steam to escape. Allow the pie to 'relax' in the refrigerator for about 1 hour.

Pre-heat the oven to gas mark 6, 400°F (200°C).

Halve the potatoes and score a deep lattice pattern on each cut surface. Brush with oil, sprinkle with garlic and season well. Place in the oven for about 1 hour, turning occasionally.

When you are ready to cook the pie, brush it with beaten egg and bake in the oven for 30–35 minutes or until golden-brown.

Prepare the sprouts and carrots and cook them in separate pans of boiling water until just tender.

Drain the carrots and reserve the cooking liquid. Put the carrots in a blender with a little of the liquid and liquidise until smooth and creamy, adding extra liquid if necessary. Return the carrot cream to its pan and re-heat, seasoning well.

Drain the sprouts. Return them to their pan, add the sunflower oil and honey and toss until the sprouts are well coated. Season well with pepper.

Serve the turkey pie on a warm platter accompanied by the vegetables.

## TASTY BUBBLE AND SQUEAK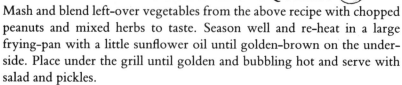

Mash and blend left-over vegetables from the above recipe with chopped peanuts and mixed herbs to taste. Season well and re-heat in a large frying-pan with a little sunflower oil until golden-brown on the under-side. Place under the grill until golden and bubbling hot and serve with salad and pickles.

# MUSHROOM HAGGIS,
*potatoes cooked in their skins and saucy leeks*

SERVES 4
*FOR THE MUSHROOM HAGGIS*
*1 tablespoon sunflower oil*
*1 large onion, peeled and chopped*
*1 large carrot, peeled and grated*
*4 oz (100 g) large flat mushrooms, chopped*
*1 teaspoon dried mixed herbs*
*1 × 7 oz (200 g) tin red kidney beans, drained*
*4 oz (100 g) split red lentils, cooked*
*2 oz (50 g) pearl barley, cooked*
*2 oz (50 g) porridge oats*
*2 teaspoons yeast extract*
*1 egg*
*Freshly ground black pepper*
*Chopped parsley to garnish*
*FOR THE POTATOES COOKED IN THEIR SKINS*
*1½ lb (750 g) unpeeled potatoes, washed and cut into even-sized pieces*
*FOR THE SAUCY LEEKS*
*2 rashers streaky bacon, rinded and diced*
*2 lb (1 kg) leeks, washed and cut into 2-inch (5-cm) pieces*
*1 × 14 oz (400 g) tin chopped tomatoes*
*Freshly ground black pepper*

Prepare a steamer for the haggis. Line the bottom of a 2-pint (1.2-litre) pudding basin with a disc of greaseproof paper and lightly grease with a little sunflower oil.

In a saucepan, heat the oil and gently fry the onion until golden–brown. Add the carrot and mushrooms and fry for a further 3 minutes. Turn the mixture into a large mixing bowl and add all the remaining haggis ingredients (except the parsley). Using a potato masher or fork, mash the ingredients together well and season to taste. Put the haggis mixture in the prepared basin, cover with a double layer of aluminium foil and tie round with string to secure. Place in the steamer and cook for 2 hours.

Thirty minutes before serving, prepare the saucy leeks. Dry-fry the bacon in a saucepan for 4 minutes, then add the leeks and cook for a further 4 minutes. Pour in the tomatoes and season to taste. Cover and simmer gently for 20 minutes.

Boil the potatoes for 15–20 minutes or until just tender.

To serve, remove the haggis from the steamer. Take off the foil and turn out on to a plate or spoon into a heated serving dish and scatter with chopped parsley. Spoon the potatoes and saucy leeks into dishes and hand separately to accompany the haggis.

# HOME-MADE SPICE PUDDING

A simple version of the traditional festive Christmas pudding.

SERVES 4
*4 oz (100 g) raisins*
*8 oz (225 g) dried apricots, chopped*
*4 oz (100 g) sultanas*
*6 oz (175 g) sunflower margarine*
*4 oz (100 g) brown sugar*
*2 eggs*
*Juice and grated rind of 2 oranges*
*2 oz (50 g) wholemeal flour*
*1 teaspoon ground cinnamon*
*1 teaspoon freshly grated nutmeg*
*8 oz (225 g) wholemeal breadcrumbs*

Grease a 2-pint (1.2-litre) pudding basin and place a piece of greaseproof paper in the bottom.

Mix the dried fruit together and set to one side.

In a large mixing bowl, beat the margarine and sugar together until soft and fluffy. Beat in the eggs and stir in the orange juice and rind. Sift the flour, spices and breadcrumbs together and add to the dried fruit in the mixing bowl. Combine thoroughly and pile into the prepared pudding basin. Cover the basin with aluminium foil and tie securely with string around the rim. Steam the pudding for 2–2½ hours or until the ingredients have fused together. When cooked, allow to stand for approximately 1 hour before serving it warm.

# RELISHES AND CHUTNEYS

When the ingredients are in season and plentiful, you can make these super fresh relishes and chutneys. The relishes are not preserved in sugar, so you should keep them in the refrigerator and eat them as soon as possible; or you could freeze them and so have them available all year round. Use them as tasty toppings for baked potatoes or with meat dishes or even to spice up gravies and stews. Whichever way you use them, they add lots of flavour to special dishes and can bring new life to everyday cooking.

## BEETROOT RELISH

MAKES 8 oz (225 g)
*2 tablespoons redcurrant jelly*
*4 tablespoons orange juice*
*1 teaspoon dried thyme*
*2 teaspoons mustard seeds*
*3 tablespoons vegetable stock or water*
*8 oz (225 g) beetroot, cooked, peeled and diced*
*½ cucumber, diced*
*1 tablespoon wholegrain mustard*
*Freshly ground black pepper*

In a small saucepan, simmer the jelly, orange juice, thyme and mustard seeds with the stock or water until reduced by half. Allow the mixture to cool, then stir in the remaining ingredients, seasoning with plenty of black pepper. Spoon the relish into a jar and serve immediately or keep covered in the refrigerator for up to 3–4 days.

# TOMATO AND APPLE RELISH

MAKES APPROX. 12 oz (350 g)
*4 large tomatoes, chopped*
*1 onion, peeled and finely chopped*
*2 eating apples, cored and finely chopped*
*FOR THE DRESSING*
*1 teaspoon mint sauce*
*1 teaspoon curry paste*
*1 tablespoon vinegar*
*2 tablespoons sunflower oil*
*Freshly ground black pepper*

In a large bowl, fork together the chopped tomatoes, onion and apples. In a smaller bowl, combine the dressing ingredients together, seasoning to taste. Pour the dressing over the tomato and apple mixture and allow to infuse for 1 hour at room temperature. Turn the relish into a bowl and serve with curries, beefburgers, barbecued dishes and salads. Store in the refrigerator and eat within 3–4 days.

# GOOSEBERRY AND RAISIN CHUTNEY

MAKES 2 lb (1 kg)
*2 lb (1 kg) gooseberries, washed and prepared*
*1 large onion, peeled and sliced*
*8 oz (225 g) raisins*
*1 tablespoon ground ginger*
*1 teaspoon ground mixed spice*
*4 oz (100 g) brown sugar*
*5 fl oz (150 ml) white vinegar*
*2 teaspoons mint sauce*
*Freshly ground black pepper*

Place the gooseberries and onion in a saucepan and cover with water. Bring to the boil, reduce the heat and simmer for 15 minutes or until soft. Stir occasionally to prevent sticking. Add the raisins, spices, sugar and vinegar and cook for a further 15–20 minutes or until thick. Stir in the mint sauce and season to taste. Spoon into warm, sterilised jars and seal. Allow to cool. Store in the fridge away from the light. Eat within 1 week.

# SPICED VEGETABLE CHUTNEY

MAKES 2 lb (1 kg)
*8 oz (225 g) red cabbage, shredded*
*1 cauliflower, broken into small florets*
*2 large parsnips, peeled and finely sliced*
*2 large tomatoes, chopped*
*1 large onion, peeled and chopped*
*4 oz (100 g) brown sugar*
*5 fl oz (150 ml) white vinegar*
*5 fl oz (150 ml) water*
*4 oz (100 g) sultanas or dried apricots*
*1 tablespoon turmeric*
*1 tablespoon curry powder*
*2 teaspoons mustard seeds*
*Freshly ground black pepper*

Parboil the cabbage, cauliflower and parsnips together in water for 5 minutes. Drain thoroughly. Add the rest of the ingredients (if using apricots, chop them) and season well. Cover and simmer on a low heat for 45 minutes–1 hour or until soft and thickish. Allow to cool, then spoon into sterilised jars and store in the refrigerator until needed and eat within 10 days. Alternatively, transfer to freezer-proof containers and freeze to keep longer.

# CHILLI CORN RELISH

MAKES 1 lb (450 g)
*1 onion, peeled and grated or finely chopped*
*2 large tomatoes, chopped*
*3 tablespoons brown sugar*
*2 teaspoons chilli sauce*
*1 × 11 oz (300 g) tin sweetcorn, drained and juice reserved*
*1 green pepper, de-seeded and finely chopped*
*Freshly ground black pepper*

Put the onion, tomatoes, brown sugar, chilli sauce and corn juice in a small saucepan. Cover and simmer over a medium heat for 4–5 minutes or until the onion has softened. Stir in the sweetcorn and chopped green pepper and allow to cool. Season well and chill for at least 2 hours. It will keep in the refrigerator for 2–3 days.

# ORANGE AND ONION RELISH

This 'salad relish' will liven up any salads you make. Unlike most fresh salads it keeps well in the fridge.

*3 large oranges*
*1 large onion, peeled and finely sliced*
*Salt and freshly ground black pepper*
*1 tablespoon sunflower oil*

Using a sharp knife, cut away the peel and pith from the oranges. Slice them across into rounds and arrange, overlapping, on a large plate. Sprinkle the onion over the oranges and season generously with salt and pepper. Trickle over the oil and allow to stand at room temperature for 30 minutes before serving. Store in the refrigerator and eat within 2–3 days.

# FRESH-FRUIT PRESERVES

Here are some simple, no-fuss instant preserves which you can whip up in no time and which can be stored in your fridge or freezer. They are ideal for cake and pie fillings or ice-cream toppings and are delicious spread on warm, crusty bread.

## WALNUT AND APPLE MARMALADE

Serve this delicious marmalade with cheese and crusty bread or salads.

MAKES 2 lb (1 kg)
*2 lb (1 kg) eating apples, cored and quartered*
*Juice and grated rind of 1 lemon*
*4 oz (100 g) brown sugar*
*½ teaspoon freshly grated nutmeg*
*4 oz (100 g) walnuts, chopped*

Put the apples and lemon juice and rind in a saucepan, stir in the sugar and then add the nutmeg. Cover with dampened greaseproof paper and a lid and cook gently until the fruit is just soft. Remove the greaseproof paper and lid and, over a fierce heat, reduce the excess liquid. Allow to cool. Add the chopped walnuts and mix well. Spoon into sterilised jars and store in the refrigerator and eat within 5–6 days.

# PEAR AND BLACKCURRANT JAM

This jam has so many uses. It goes with bread, cakes, scones and cheese. It can also add flavour to sauces, stews and soups.

MAKES 2 lb (1 kg)
*2 lb (1 kg) pears, cored and cut into chunks*
*1 tablespoon runny honey*
*Juice and grated rind of 1 large orange*
*8 oz (225 g) blackcurrants, prepared*

Place the pears, honey and orange juice and rind in a saucepan and cook, covered, over a gentle heat for about 50 minutes–1 hour or until the fruit is soft, glossy and transparent. Add the blackcurrants, mix well and remove from the heat. Allow to cool. Spoon into sterilised jars and store in the refrigerator. Eat within 1 week, or freeze.

# PLUM CHEESE

This wonderful mixture may be served on toast, warm oatcakes or crusty bread. It could also be used as a topping for scones and pancakes.

MAKES 1½ lb (750 g)
*2 lb (1 kg) plums, halved and stoned*
*4 oz (100 g) sultanas*
*1 teaspoon ground cinnamon*
*1 tablespoon porridge oats*

Place all the ingredients in a saucepan together with a little water. Cover with dampened greaseproof paper and a lid and simmer for 10–15 minutes or until the plums are just soft. Allow the mixture to cool. Spoon into sterilised jars and store in the refrigerator. Eat within 4–5 days.

# GOOSEBERRY JAM

Serve with toast or oatcakes, or as a topping for porridge or cereals.

MAKES 1½ lb (750 g)
*2 lb (1 kg) gooseberries, washed and prepared*
*1 teaspoon ground ginger*
*5 fl oz (150 ml) orange or apple juice*
*1 bay leaf*
*4 oz (100 g) brown sugar*

Place all the ingredients in a large saucepan, cover and cook until the gooseberries are soft. Remove the lid and evaporate the excess liquid over a fierce heat. Allow the mixture to cool fully. Store in the refrigerator and eat within 4–5 days, or freeze.

# DRESSINGS

Liven up salads and vegetables with these tasty dressings. Made 1–2 hours in advance, the flavours will have time to develop.

## CUCUMBER DRESSING

*½ cucumber, liquidised*
*1 tablespoon lemon juice*
*1 teaspoon mint sauce*
*1 tablespoon fromage frais*
*Freshly ground black pepper*

Combine the ingredients in a mixing bowl, seasoning to taste.

# HORSERADISH DRESSING

*1 tablespoon horseradish sauce*
*1 carrot, scrubbed and grated*
*1 tablespoon fromage frais*
*1 tablespoon orange juice*
*1 teaspoon chilli sauce*
*Freshly ground black pepper*

Liquidise the ingredients together and season to taste.

# SPICY DRESSING

*1 clove garlic, peeled and crushed*
*1 tablespoon sunflower oil*
*4 tablespoons natural yoghurt*
*1 teaspoon curry paste*
*½ teaspoon ground ginger*
*Freshly ground black pepper*

Combine the ingredients and season to taste.

# ZINGY DRESSING

*2 spring onions, finely chopped*
*3 tablespoons grapefruit juice*
*1 teaspoon runny honey*
*1 teaspoon dried thyme*
*3 tablespoons sunflower oil*
*Freshly ground black pepper*

Mix the ingredients well in a bowl and season to taste.

# TOMATO AND GARLIC DRESSING

*5 fl oz (150 ml) tomato juice*
*1 tomato, finely chopped*
*1 teaspoon French mustard*
*1 clove garlic, peeled and crushed*
*1 teaspoon dried oregano*
*1 tablespoon soy sauce*
*1 tablespoon fromage frais (optional)*
*Freshly ground black pepper*

Combine the ingredients and season to taste.

# MUSTARD SEED DRESSING

*1 tablespoon wholegrain mustard*
*2 teaspoons poppy seeds*
*1 apple, cored and grated*
*5 fl oz (150 ml) orange or apple juice*
*1 tablespoon sunflower oil*
*Freshly ground black pepper*

Mix the ingredients thoroughly in a bowl and season to taste.

# SWEET SAUCES AND SORBETS

Fromage frais and natural yoghurt are great, healthy alternatives to cream to serve with your puddings. However, if you fancy a change, try these easy and tasty sauces.

A great advantage of the fruity sauces is that they can be made into wonderful sorbets. Simply blend them to a purée, place in the freezer until half-frozen, whisk in a couple of beaten egg whites and return to the freezer until just hard.

## EASY CUSTARD SAUCE

SERVES 4
*15 fl oz (450 ml) semi-skimmed milk*
*Juice and grated rind of 1 orange*
*½ teaspoon freshly grated nutmeg*
*1 tablespoon cornflour*
*2 teaspoons brown sugar*
*2–3 drops vanilla essence*

In a saucepan, gently heat together the milk, orange rind and nutmeg and bring to the boil. In a cup, blend the cornflour with the orange juice and brown sugar and pour this into the boiling milk. Whisk well and simmer for 2–3 minutes. Then cool the custard slightly and add the vanilla essence. Serve the sauce hot or cold.

# SPICED CREAM

SERVES 4
1 teaspoon ground cinnamon
½ teaspoon freshly grated nutmeg
¼ teaspoon ground ginger
1 dessertspoon runny honey
9 oz (250 g) fromage frais

In a small saucepan, dry-fry the spices for 30 seconds. Remove the pan from the heat and stir in the honey. Allow to cool, then stir in the fromage frais. Spoon into a bowl and chill before serving.

# APRICOT SAUCE

This is also good made with peaches instead of apricots.

SERVES 4
1 × 14 oz (400 g) tin apricots in natural juice
5 fl oz (150 ml) orange juice
½ teaspoon freshly grated nutmeg

Liquidise the apricots and their juice, the orange juice and nutmeg until smooth. Serve warm or cold.

# RED SUMMER SAUCE

SERVES 4
12 oz (350 g) mixed soft red summer fruits (such as strawberries,
raspberries and redcurrants)
Runny honey to taste

Blend the fruits together until puréed and add honey to taste. Serve chilled.

# INDEX

Italics indicate recipes where any left-overs provide the basis for another dish.

# INDEX

# INDEX